CAPELLA DE GERARDEGILE.

GARRIGILL VILLAGE,

SHEWING THE CHURCH, PARSONAGE, CHURCH ROOM, AND GLEBE.

Opp. the Title.

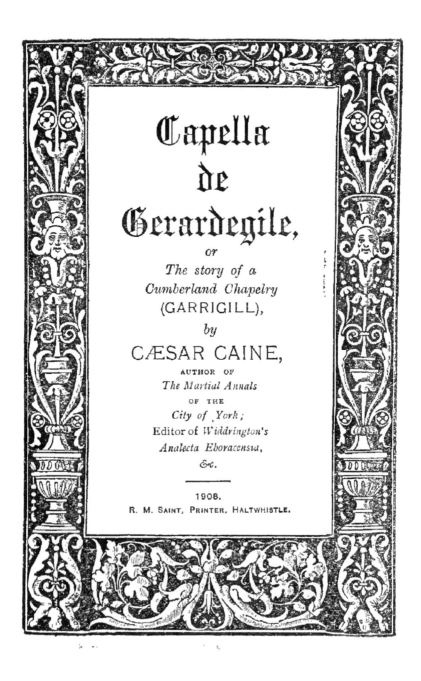

Capella de Gerardegile,

or

The story of a
Cumberland Chapelry
(GARRIGILL),

by

CÆSAR CAINE,

AUTHOR OF

The Martial Annals

OF THE

City of York ;

Editor of *Widdrington's*

Analecta Eboracensia,

&c.

1908.

R. M. SAINT, PRINTER, HALTWHISTLE.

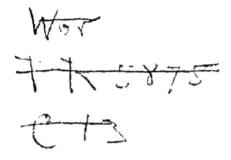

To The Memory of
ELIZABETH,
My Dear Mother:
A True Daughter
OF
"Canny Cummerlan'.'

TABLE OF CONTENTS.

—.o:——

LIST OF ILLUSTRATIONS.

——:o.——

INTRODUCTION.

This book is a record of *The Church* in Garrigill. Other matters are only introduced so far as they assist, or are related to, the ecclesiastical story.

The introduction is written chiefly to justify such a limitation of our subject.

In entering upon a historical enquiry about a parish, one's thoughts turn instinctively, in the first place, to Domesday Book. Professor Maitland says:—*

"A place that is mentioned in Domesday Book will probably be recognised as a *vill* in the thirteenth century, and a civil parish in the nineteenth century. Let us take Cambridgeshire by way of example. Excluding the Isle of Ely, we find that the political geography of the Conqueror's reign has endured until our time The boundaries of the hundreds lie almost where they lay, the number of *vills* has hardly been increased or diminished. About one hundred and ten *vills* that were *vills* in 1086 are vills or civil

---

Domesday Book and Beyond, pub. 1897, p 12,

parishes at the present day, and in all probability they then had approximately the same boundaries that they have now."

It is a source of constant disappointment to the student that Domesday Book furnishes practically no record of the northern extremity of our country. The reason for this deficiency is apparent at once. " When the successive disorders and devastations of these northern parts, during the Conqueror's reign, are considered, it is not to be wondered at that there is no account of Northumberland, Cumberland, and Westmoreland in the famous Domesday Book, which contains a particular survey of all the parts of England, and was finished the year before the Conqueror's death "*

We must, therefore, be content with documentary evidence of a later date.

1.—The mountain Chapelry of Garrigill has had the good fortune to belong to a mother Church which, as a dependency of the important Abbey of Hexham, has a well-preserved history. The Black Book (*Liber Niger*) of Hexham is a rent roll of The Abbey compiled in the XV Century. Here we find extended references to Alston and Garrigill. These records, it must be

---

* Ridpath (George and Phillip), The Border History of England and Scotland. MDCCCX.

borne in mind, represent a state of things of much earlier date than the age of The Black Book itself. Under the heading LIBERTAS DE TYNDALE CUM PRESDALE ET ALDEN-NESTON MORE* there are two interesting references to Garrigill.

The first extract is brief, which I translate† as follows:—

"They hold also in Gerard-gill one toft‡ which is called Thruswell, and they hold also in the same place pasture for ten cows and two mares with all their issue up to two years of age."

The second extract is more lengthy than the previous one.

"PRESDALE.—They hold also all Presdale and its several parts § the whole year round; and if any shall have used the grazing with any beasts, at any time, within the divisions of the pasture of Presdale he ought to be apprehended before the Court of the Prior of the same and justify himself. And Presdale is contained within these divisions:—Beginning under Eshgill head, just as the water-shed divideth, as far as Edestone:

---

*Surtees Society. Priory of Hexham, Vol ii., p 15.
† For the Latin text see Appendix K.
‡ A place where a house formerly stood.
§ It was a joint tenancy—singly and severally

And thence as far as Burnhope Head by Hard Road, as the water divideth as far as Brownspot (Burnpot) Lane;

And thence as far as Crook Burn Head, and by the same Crook Burn as far as the River Tees;

And thence from the entrance of Crook Burn into the Tees, by ascending as far as the top of Fiends' Fell;

And thence in a straight line to Wakstone Edge;

And thence as far as the spring at Cashwell wane;

And thence across the bog, East ward, as far as Nunstones;

And thence as far as Cokeley Fell;

And thence, descending by Eller Burn as far as the River Tyne;

And so, by the Tyne as far as Eshgill Foot;

And thence, ascending by Eshgill as far as Eshgill Head first named.*

They have also free ingress, transit, and exit, throughout the whole fee of Alston, to the aforesaid Presdale, without hindrance on the part of anyone, and also for the men of the aforesaid

---

* "The form in which [such] boundaries are given is of great antiquity. It is a form used by the Romans 2000 years ago, and almost continuously followed from that time to this." Seebohm, *English Village Community,* p 9.

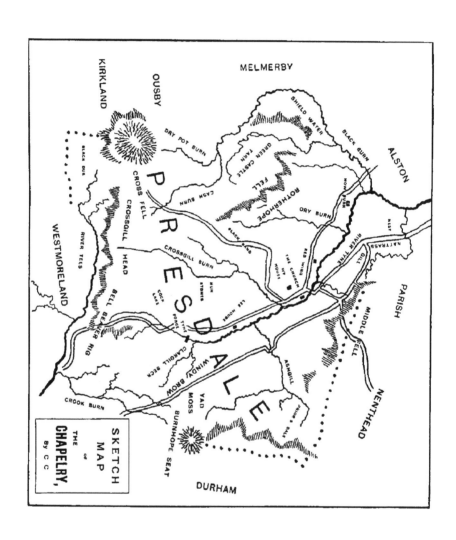

MELMERBY

KIRKLAND

OUSBY

ALSTON

WESTMORELAND

DRY POT BURN

SHIELD WATER

BLACK BURN

GREEN CASTLE FARN

MOOR BURN

CROSS FELL

CROSSGILL HEAD

RIVER TEES

BLACK BUR

CASH BURN

ROTHERHOPE FELL

DRY BURN

P R E S D A L E

CROSSGILL BURN

BLACK BURN

THE CHURCH

IVY HOUSE

RED WING

BELL BEAVER RIG

COCK LAKE

RUN STONES

TEES HOUSE

RIVER TYNE

NATTRASS

NEST

RIVER TYNE

NATTRASS GILL

PARISH

MIDDLE FELL

WINDY BROW

YAD MOSS

ASHGILL

NENTHEAD

CROOK BURN

CLARGILL BECK

BURNHOPE SEAT

TEES HEAD

BURNHOPE SEAT

DURHAM

SKETCH MAP OF THE CHAPELRY, BY C C

Prior and Convent, and for their animals of every kind; neither shall they be challenged (let them be) or disturbed, whether going or coming (returning or crossing) by causing delay, by day or by night, in the pasture of Alston, with their cattle, outside the divisions of Presdale first named.

And the aforesaid Prior and (members of) the Convent have the right of communication through all the pasture of Alston-moor, with all their animals going out of Presdale, every day, just as they please, from sun rise to sun set, without any interference whatsoever."

"LIBERTIES AND EASEMENTS BELONGING TO PRESDALE IN ALDENESTON MORE.

The aforesaid Prior and Convent, and their dependents (homines) dwelling in the town-land of Aldneston, have rights of cutting timber in the woods of Aldneston for building purposes, and for keeping their houses and fences in repair, and for all other necessary purposes, according as they have need, without let or hindrance on the part of any one whatsoever.

They hold also in the town land of Chesterhope in Redesdale two tofts and two crofts, which crofts, indeed, together with the tofts, lie side by side. Moreover, in the middle of the town land on the south side of the ford, in the path which leads to the common pasture, lying on the north side of the said path, they hold also two bovates,* called one husband land,† containing twelve acres each, like the rest of the husband lands in the same town land, that is to say twenty-four acres.

And they lay waste for nearly forty years; and all mutual charges are paid in a lump sum at the end of every ten years, by paying thence (i e. from these lands) the yearly sum of ten shillings.

And from this land (inde) is remitted to Adam de Lee who holds the same, through the Prior at his ‡ (the Prior's) good will, and by service,§ for every year to the end of the term of the aforesaid ten years, the sum of six shillings and eightpence.

---

* Bovate or Oxgang: Land ploughed by a team of oxen.

† The Prior and Convent of Hexham divided out their lands between tenants of three kinds . farmers, husband-men, and cottagers   A husband-land varied from twelve to thirty-four acres (Black Book, Preface, xix)   The best land was let in the smallest quantities   The husband-land of Presdale was a medium quantity- twenty-four.

‡ One of the houses at Tynehead still preserves the name of *Lee*—Lee House, anciently called Le Lee.   See p. 107, 162, 164, and 192.

§ That is, the service of Adam Lee

And so he pays clear during the same years the sum of three shillings and fourpence."*

These two extracts show that this obscure village had a very definite relationship to the Augustinian monastary at Hexham, the erection of which was one of the great triumphs of Archbishop Wilfrid's restless life.

This possession of the Monastery was given to the Prior and Brethren by Ivo, son of William de Veteri Ponte, to be held in " frank almoigne " Though this grant was confirmed by the sovereign power, its validity was afterwards challenged. A writ was issued against the Priory of Hexham for usurping a franchise belonging to the King.

The records of the trial are dated at Carlisle and York, and issued in the establishment of the claim of Hexham Priory to the Estate.

In the pleadings in these trials is said to comprise over 2,000 acres. There is some error here, for the perambulation given above contains an area of nearly four times that acreage. Part of these Abbey-lands are known to this day as Prior's Dale.

It now remains to enquire what befell this property at the dissolution of the monasteries.

---

* 10s. minus 6s. 8d. is 3s. 4d. Adam Lee pays this balance to the Prior.

Hodgson says that prior to the dissolution of the religious houses the Prior's Dale Estate was leased to one George Lawson, who, in the reign of Queen Elizabeth, obtained a grant of it in fee Subsequently his son, Thomas, conveyed it, in three large selections, to various owners. This division took place in 1588.

1. Eshgill passed into the hands of Arthur Jackson and Henry Renwick.* This parcel changed hands several times and for more than twenty years has belonged to a mining company.

2. The Hole property was conveyed to Nicholas and Anthony Walton. After various vicissitudes it passed in 1851 to the Greenwich Hospital.

3. The remainder of the Presdale area (the larger part, being known as The Hill Liberty) was conveyed to John Whitfield.

Until quite recently this property was held by the family of Colonel A. M. Cranmer Byng. It has now passed into the hands of Mr. R. Todd of Alston.

11. A discussion of Garrigill place names in general would be beyond the scope of this book But we cannot overlook the fact that the highest

---

* See Appendix L

point in the district bears ecclesiastical names.

As we have already seen, a very large part of the eastern side of Cross Fell lies within the boundaries of the Chapelry. The two names of this mountain—so different, and indeed so contrary—preserve an ecclesiastical fable, which, though worthless in itself, is full of interest to the student of folk-lore. The legend is well known. Wallace, in his MS. notes, quotes a writer of the beginning of the xviii Century, who relates the story in these words:—

"It was formerly called Fiends' Fell from evil spirits which are said in former times to have haunted the summit of the hill, and continued their haunts and nocturnal vagaries upon it, until St. Austin, as it is said, erected a cross and an altar whereon he offered the Holy Eucharist by which he counter-charmed those hellish fiends and broke their haunts.

Since that time it has borne the name of Cross Fell, and to this day there is a heap of stones which goes by the name of The Altar upon the Fell."

No one acquainted with the summit of Cross Fell can wonder that, in less enlightened ages, weird legends should be associated with the spot.

Those who have reached the mountain top, even

in summer, and have been overtaken by an enveloping mist, or even by a haze, when all the
distance has been blotted out and the summit has
appeared like an island instead of a hill, or have
been assailed suddenly by the strong winds which
whistle and scream among the grasses and stones,
must have felt their surroundings to be uncanny in
the highest degree

What wonder if in the old days people believed
that the region was the home of demons?

This is the simple and reasonable explanation of
the appellation " Fiends' Fell." Sir Edward Burne-
Jones very effectively describes such a landscape,
when he expresses his disappointment at some
southern scenes He says " Everybody smiles fat
smiles at the big green carpet It seems churlish
not to admire it It is bonny, but I like other
lands better, and now and then I want to see *Hell*
in a landscape "

I think that the term " Cross" is capable of an
explanation equally sane and easy.

It was customary to erect crosses on summits by
the side of mountain passes.

Thus we have—Hartside Cross, Long Cross, Blacklow Cross, Kilhope Cross, Short's Cross, and Middle
Cleugh Cross.

Doubtless a cross was erected on Fiends' Fell by the side of the old Garrigill Pass.* The term Cross Fell would then distinguish this pass from other passes over the Pennine Hills.

III —The derivation of the original name Gerardegile (Gerard's Ghyll), afterwards contracted to Garrigill is almost too obvious to require any notice † But it is interesting to note how the name Gerard has been associated with other localities. There is a Gerard's Acre in Essex (Claus. Rot 29 Ed 1, mem 17). In 1691 £2,343 of the King's money was stolen from a wagon at Gerard's Cross, Bucks (Cal. Treasury Papers 1557—1696). Gerardedale in Helmsley was granted by Everard de Ros to Rievaux Abbey in the 12th Century (Chart of Rievaux). This by no means exhausts a list I have made casually in the course of my reading.

IV.—It is extremely difficult to separate the interests of Alston and Garrigill.

The advowson of Alston was held by the Prior of Hexham, and, of course, Garrigill, as a dependent Chapelry, recognised the same authority.

For instance, in the Charter Rolls of Henry III (Nov. 21, 1232, at Northampton) there is a Grant‡

---

* Vide p 108.   † Vide p. 3

‡ This is really a confirmation   The gift was made very early in xiii Century, and confirmed by King John (Hodgson). Later the Grant was confirmed again by Edward I.   Vide Rot Cart. 34 Ed. I, also Memorials of Hexham, Voll. ii, p 119.   There are earlier presentations. See p 23.

to St. Andrew of Hextıldesham and the Regular
Canons there . . . .
" of the gift of the same Ivo (Veterı Ponte) th e
advowson of the Church of Aldenıston *with the
Chapel of Gerardegıll* "

In 1296, Hexham, and much of the South Tyne
valley, was devastated by the ferocıous Scots   The
records, charters, and other documents of the
Monastery perıshed by fire. Immedıately after thıs
mısfortune a commıssıon was appoınted to ratıfy
the possessıons of the Prıor. The fındıngs of the
commıssıon were embodıed ın a Great Charter,
which ranks ın importance, in the Annals of the
Abbey, next to The Black Book   John Hodgson *
prınted thıs charter, but the copy he followed was
very untrustworthy   It may be read ın its entırety
in the Annals of Hexham (Surtees Socıety).† Thıs
important document refers to Presdale, or Prıorsdale
" They hold also a certaın pasture, whıch ıs called
Presdale, wıth ıts belongıngs, by ıts proper dıvısıons,
in its several (parts) ın free, sımple, and perpetual
benefactıon, of the gift of Ivo de Veterı   Ponte,
and from that tıme they have held a charter and
confırmatıon of the sovereıgn lord, Kıng Henry,
father of the sovereıgn lord, the Kıng that now ‡ ıs,

---

* The Hıstory of Northumberland, Vol. ıı, Pt. 3, pp.
156 –170.

† Prıory of Hexham, Vol ıı, p 107.

‡ Edward I, 1272—1307.

and they have held this from a time to which the memory (of man) does not extend."*

It is important to notice in connection with the changes which have taken place in the advowson that the Alston Estates passed by purchase into the hands of the Radcliffes of Dilston. Because of the part taken by James Radcliffe, the last Earl of Derwentwater, in the rebellion of 1715, the estates were forfeited to the crown. In 1735 these estates were settled upon Greenwich Hospital, and are now administered by The Admiralty

These and many other similar facts have a direct bearing upon Garrigill, but they cannot be dealt with in detail because they belong more particularly to the history of the superior and mother Church at Alston.

This statement will explain why other important local matters are only referred to *in passim* in these pages.

V.—To speak of the ancient industry of the district—lead mining—is no part of my proper task. On page 16 I give an interesting fact showing a connection between the Mines and the Church. To insert one or two general facts may not, however be out of place here.

---

* For the Latin text see Appendix M

(1) The records of this industry begin at a very early date. In *Eulogium Historiarum** we have "ET ANNO MCXXXIII VENA ARGENTARIA INVENTA EST KARLILLE" But the Pipe Roll† shews that these mines were worked years before 1133 (2) The mines of Alston area were recorded at the Exchequer as the Mines of *Carlisle* ‡ (3) These Mines are strangely spoken of as the King's *silver* mines though their impregnation by this more precious metal was of a very low degree.

VI —The perusal of private papers has brought to light one or two facts about "The Chapel" which are missing among the Church papers. The earliest repairs, of the present building, are given on p 29, as carried out in 1752 But there were earlier repairs executed in 1746 for John Archer then contributed to that object. Again, the list of Church Wardens begins in 1737 (Vide p. 75) But William Archer was Chapel Warden five years before, 1732.§

On page 80 we have "Town-meadow Heads" These lands to-day are spoken of as "Tongue-meadow Heads" But the Redwing Register also

---

* (Rolls Series) III, p, 64 (Edited F. S. Haydon)
† Hen. I. Rot. 14 dorso.
‡ Claus. Rot. 30 Ed. III, m. 16 , Pat. Rot. 2 Hen. V. p 2 m 13 Inquis. ad Quod Damnum, 3 Hen. V, No. 7.
§ Vide Pedigree, p. 168.

has "Townmeadow Heads" like the Church books. The list on page 91 displays the names of the defaulters. The Magistrates names were A. Huddeston and J. Richardson. These were not on my copy.

VII.—In making a collection, and then a selection of materials for this history, a large mass of information has come into my hands, including copies of scores of wills, which, however valuable, and interesting cannot be used in these pages. Some items belong wholly to Alston, and others are without any special bearing on the religious life of the people. As illustrating I give two extracts haphazard. Pat. Rolls. 8 Rich. II, p. 2, m. 11 Westminster, May 6: Pardon granted to Richard son of John Ibben of Alstone, for the death of William Bust, killed before the Invention of The Cross, 7 Rich. II. Close Rolls, 20 Ed. III, p 2, m 16, 1346 Oct. 12: Order to the Sheriff of Cumberland. To cause a Coronor for that county to be elected in the place of William le Taillour of Auldstonmore who does not stay in the county and has no lands there whereof he can answer the king and his people in accordance with the statute.

More than one attempt has been made to write a general history of Alston, but this is a work which has still to be attempted. Only a diligent searcher among the archives of our country can form any conception of the wealth of material which awaits the worker who is prepared to put time, and money, and love into this enterprize

VIII —Lately, but after long delay, a MS. collection made by William Wallace, author of Alston Moor, has been placed, according to his will, in the Mechanics' Institute, Alston.

These papers contain nothing new in relation to Garrigill. I have abstracted one or two notes, from a second copy, and have duly acknowledged their origin

IX.—At present Church life in the Chapelry is buoyant and vigorous. Lately, £120 has been spent upon improving the Church estate, and an entire renovation of the interior of the Church building is now projected Much is being done also for the people on social lines.

X —May I add one personal word. A backward glance upon my life at Garrigill is like the remembrance of a beautiful dream. I never knew so much real happiness in my life before Sometimes I think I shall never know such happiness here again. The deep religiousness, the transparent honesty, the loving sympathy of the people were such as I have never intimately experienced elsewhere. Nor must I fail to mention the charm of their speech, full of grand old English words long since forgotten by the town dwellers, and often enriched with impromptu metaphors which reminded me of the lesser images of the Hebrew prophets !

And then, the place !

"Sing, hey for the moorlands, wild, lonely, and stern,
Where the moss creepeth softly all under the fern;
Where the heather-flower sweetens the lone highland lea,
And the mountain winds whistle so fresh and so free!
I've wandered o'er landscapes embroidered with flowers,
The richest, the rarest, in greenest of bowers,
Where the 'throstle's' sweet vesper at summer day's close,
Shook the coronal dews on the rim of the rose;
But, oh for the hills where the heather-cock springs
From the nest in the bracken, with dew on his wings!
I've lingered by steamlets that water green plains,
I've mused in the sunlight of shady old lanes,
Where the mild breath of evening came sweetly and slow
From green rocks where bluebells and primroses grow;
But, oh the wild hills that look up at the skies,
Where the green brackens wave to the wind as its flies!"

CÆSAR CAINE.

Ipswich, 1908.

CHAPTER I.

THE REMOTE PAST—HISTORY IN NAMES.

A T the south-eastern extremity of Cumberland, where the South Tyne finds its source, and beneath the shadow of Cross Fell (2,989 ft.) the highest point of the Pennine Range, there lies a mountain village clustering round a plain but interesting old Church, known in the documents of our nation, nearly a thousand years ago, as *Capella de Gerardegile.*

Our first documentary information belongs to the XII. century. But the district has an earlier history which has perished almost without a memorial, except in its name.

Of the period anterior to the Roman occupation of our country (A.D. 100-412) we have hardly any grounds even for

B

conjecture. The few stone implements, which have been found here, suggest that if the Ancient Britons had no permanent settlement in this upper part of the South Tyne valley, they visited the district either for the purpose of hunting, or of feeding their flocks.

The Romans must have been acquainted with the neighbourhood, for a Roman road runs right across one corner of Alston parish, of which Garrigill is part. Close to Alston, and within five miles of Garrigill village, there is the site of a Roman camp, which was visited by Dr. Bruce during his investigations into northern Roman antiquities. Indeed, at Tynehead, within the Chapelry, there is a field known as the Chesters. It seems to me that the site is not void of evidences of occupation in the remote past, and I have been told by an old resident that when he was a youth coins and other articles were discovered in this field. But of this period we have now practically no information.

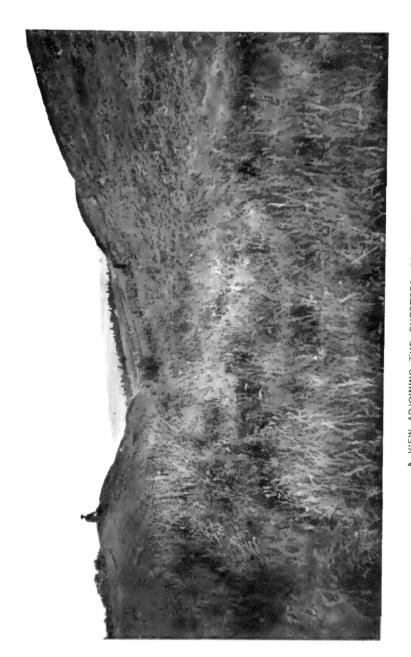

A VIEW ADJOINING THE CHESTERS, GARRIGILL.

Opp. p. 2.

From the sonorous cognomen the district bears we know that the Anglo-Saxons must have had a colony here long before the Norman Conquest (1066).

"Garrigill" is a compound of two words—Gerard, the name of a Saxon adventurer, and Gill (a contraction of Ghyll), meaning a hope, or dene, or glen. "Garrigill," when translated, becomes "The Valley of Gerard"

In the Church Register the name of the village is spelt Garragill, the second vowel being *a*, not *i*. This second *a* is less of a corruption—though it looks unfamiliar if not unwelcome—than the modern i—Garrigill. It would seem that the second *a* in Garragill is the second *a* of Gerard. "Garragill," then, is purer than "Garrigill." I find that Palmer adopts the form Garragill throughout in *The Tyne and its Tributaries.*

But Garrigill has another name, and this, too, is Anglo-Saxon. I find Garrigill called in the old registers "Gate." The head and foot of the village are called respectively Gate-head, and Gate-foot, among the people of the place to this day.

Four different solutions of this name have been advocated.

1. I have heard it suggested that a gate once barred the highway here. This I consider an impossible solution of the word.

2. "Gate" signifies a way. This sense is preserved in such a phrase as "Gang yer ain gate "(Go your own way), or "Sair trouble cam' our gate" (Sore trouble came our way). Now, Garrigill is the only village on the way to the mines and moors between Alston and Middleton-in-Teesdale, and it is also the route and land-mark for all persons making for Crossfell, the great feature of the whole district. It has been suggested that in this way Garrigill became known as "Gate," or The Way. This theory also needs no confutation.

3. Again, it is said Garrigill is really a long *street*, as compared with many of the meagre and shapeless villages of this mountain region, and thus it became known as " Gat," " Gata," or " Street."

But to this it may be replied that the name " Gate " is given to several places in the vicinity which possess no pretentions to being a street—*e.g.*, Bleagate, and Gossipgate.

4. The right theory is this. There are pastures wherein two or three persons have " grassings"—*i.e.*, liberty to feed so many cattle, for a set period. The old word for " grassing " is " stint." A man might have three " stints " in a certain area of grass—the right to feed three cows, but only three. There is still an older word than " grassing " or " stint," meaning exactly the same thing—"geat."

In " cattle-geat " a cow was the standard. Five black-faced sheep were a " geat " and three Leicesters were the same. A cart-horse was two " geats."

It is easily understood how the word "geat" came to mean a proportion of cattle. The word, as we have seen, meant originally a street or enclosure. In an area used by several farmers, where there were no sub-divisions in the form of walls or dykes, the division had to be made by counting heads of cattle. Thus the measurement was in time transferred from the land to the beasts feeding upon it. "Geat" meant an enclosure, and it came to mean a unit of grazing stock.

Garrigill, surrounded on every side by the wild fells, was the most valuable pasture near the source of the South Tyne. The whole of the flat land forming the village proper was occupied, therefore, by the ancient dwellers here on the "geat" system. So Garrigill, because of its pastures, became "Gate."

The village, then, has two names, Garrigill, the common name; and Gate, used locally. Both words are pure Anglo-

Saxon, and present the clearest evidence that the foundation of the present community was an Anglo-Saxon colony.

CHAPTER II.

NORMAN DAYS—A HISTORIC FAMILY.

FROM the remote days to which we have referred until now, the people of Garrigill, shut in on every side by the great hills, have lived a life much isolated from the outside world—so much so that they use daily many words which we are familiar with only because we see them crystalized in the Bible, the Book of Common Prayer, and the old English classics.

They employ many forms of speech used by their forefathers three and four hundred years ago. Much of what sounds in the ears of visitors as "provincialisms" is strong idiomatic English. These and similar considerations invest the place and the people with a fascinating interest.

I have looked upon the mountains in winter. The snow-patches have been dull and chalk-like. The stone-walls have been ugly in spite of the mosses which so kindly cover them.

But now the western sun is setting with a glow like molten metal.

Look at the mountain now!

Its snowy cap is suffused with the daintiest shade of rose-pink. The ugly walls are glorified into piles of shining bronze and gold. The wild mountain-side is something to dream about for the rest of your life.

Similarly as I have seen the bright beams of historic lore fall on this northern valley, and its plain, sturdy, laborious people—true children of the land in which they live—they have appeared almost transfigured.

In imagination I have seen the place peopled with its ancient inhabitants, and my village neighbours have appeared rich in the inheritance of a long strenuous, and heroic past.

I shall devote this chapter to the early records of an ancient family of the neighbourhood—the Viponds

The Barons Veteri Ponte—the name appears as early as 1085—had considerable possessions in the north. To one branch of this family Garrigill (with other lands) belonged. The old Norman name is perpetuated in the village in the form of " Vipond "   .

The following facts refer to the period immediately succeeding the Norman Conquest :—

1. The parishes of Alston-cum-Garrigill, Knarsdale, Kirkhaugh, Whitfield, Simonburn, and part of Haltwhistle formed the Franchise of Tynedale, and were held by the King of Scotland from the King of England.

2. The Manor of Alston and other lands were given to William de Veteri Ponte by William the Lion, King of Scotland. This grant was confirmed by King John on May 10, 1209.

HEXHAM ABBEY.

3. Ivo de Veteri Ponte transferred the advowson of the Church of Alston and the Chapel at Garrigill to Hexham Abbey.

4. The son of Ivo was Robert. Edward I (1272-1307) recovered from Robert Veteri Ponte the Manor of Alston. It was afterwards restored to the Scotch King. In 1279 (June 21) the Sheriff of Cumberland was ordered to restore to Alexander, King of Scotland, his liberty of Aldeston, which the Sheriff took into the King's hands by order of the Justices in Eyre in that county (vide Claus. Rot. 7, Ed. I. Mem. 6).

5. The Manor was restored to Nicholas de Veteri Ponte in 1282.

There is a grant—dated July 4 in that year, at the instance of the King of Scotland—to Nicholas, son of Robert de Veteri Ponte that he may hold the Manor of Aldeneston, which the King of England lately recovered, as of his county of Cumberland, by judgment of the King's Court, against the said Robert—saving, however,

to the King and his heirs the mine of
Aldeneston, the miners, and the liberty of
the same : and also that the said Manor
shall henceforth belong to the King of
Scotland's liberty of 'Tindall, provided that
the miners shall answer to the King for
the said mines, as hitherto (vide Pat. Rot.
10, Ed. I., Mem. 9).

There is an "Inspeximus" of this grant,
dated Jan. 22, in 1334 (vide Pat. Rot. 7,
Ed. III. Pars. ii., Mem. 3).

6.   Nicholas appears to have been de-
prived again, for there is an order—made
at York, Oct. 10, 1314—to John de Evre,
Escheator, "this side of Trent," to deliver
to John de Whelpdale, the custody, during
pleasure, of the Manor of Aldeston, which
belonged to Nicholas de Vepunt, so that
he should answer to the Exchequer for
the issues of the same (vide Claus. Rot. 8
Ed. II., Mem. 31).

7.   Within the year (1315, or 8, Ed. II.)
Nicholas died, but appears to have come
again into his possession of the Alston
Manor.

By Inquest it was found that he held, at the time of his death, "the capital messuage in Alderstone, and that he had thirty-three tenants " in Gerardgile who held twenty-three shieldings (vide Cal. Inquis. post mortem, 8 Ed. II., No. 20).

8. I find another interesting reference to this family in Nov. 2nd, 1337.

License was granted for Robert de Vicupont to impark his wood of Walne-wood in Aldneston, provided that it be not within the metes of the King's forest (vide Pat. Rot. 11, Ed. III., Pars. iii., Mem. 18).

9. These lands, with others, remained in possession of this family until 1443.

---

* The printed Index to the Calendar is wrong. It says " 23 tenements."

CHAPTER III

MINES—SCOTS—SOCIAL LIFE.

THE Public Records—from which I have culled the paragraphs which form the previous chapter—abound with items which, in different ways, throw light upon the life of these people in early days.

Three facts especially find interesting and valuable illustration from this source —the life of the people as lead miners, their insecurity owing to the constant raids of the Scotch, and the feuds which are always common among a primitive and strong-minded people.

1. Reference has already been made to the mining industry of the neighbourhood (p. 12).

There is another very interesting reference of this kind in March 23, 1475.

In that year there was granted to the King's brother—Richard, Duke of Gloucester; the King's kinsman—Henry, Earl of Northumberland; William Goderswyk, merchant, and others—certain mines. . One of these is familar to every child in Garrigill to-day, though it is now silent and unworked. It is described as "the mine in Alston More, called Feccheroos" (vide Pat. Rot. 15, Ed. IV , Pars. i., Mem. 22).

In a document of about the same date it is spelt "Fleccheroos" (vide Pat. Rot. 15, Ed. IV., Pars. i., Mem. 12).

This mine is situate on the hillside, on the left, at the entrance of Garrigill village, approaching from Alston; and the name is corrupted to-day into "Fletcheras" and "Fletchers." When I first went to Garrigill I thought "Fletchers" referred to some modern speculator, who had owned the rights of this mine.

Fletcheras *alias* Fleccheroos Mine has been a busy centre of mining operations within the memory of many living in Garrigill to-day.

One interesting item in the grant of March, 1475, was that one-tenth part of the "lees ewrs" issuing from the mine should be paid "to the Curate of the place."

2   We now pass on to notice the disquiet and insecurity caused by the Scots.

The troubles caused by the Scots were so severe and of so long duration that they tincture the habits and lives of the people of these once plundered valleys, even to this day.

(a) In 1334 there was a confirmation of Letters Patent, dated Feb., 7, Henry III. (1216-1272), being a protection for the King's miners at Aldeneston, granted at the request of the miners, as the original letters had been *burned by the Scots* (Pat. Rot. 8, Ed. III., Pars. ii., Mem. 21).

There is another very significant fact mentioned in the Patent Rolls, under date 1344.   In the 14th year of Edward III. (1327-1377) the North was so ravaged and plundered by the Scots that the people of

Aldeston Moor were not able to pay the King's dues (18 Ed. III., Pars. ii., Mem. 22, dorso).

(b) The men of the South Tyne Valley were not only called upon to defend their homes on their native soil, but were pressed to take up arms, and serve at a distance, against their restless foe.

King Edward I. (1272-1307) died near Carlisle on July 7, 1307. His presence here was owing to a threatened invasion of the Scots. Often had he defeated them; twice it seemed he had conquered them. But, at the age of almost seventy, he was obliged to take the field again.

In the previous February Edward was at Lanercost Abbey, and he issued a summons to Robert Tymparon, Adam de Whiteberough, John de Stafful, and Nicholas de Harleston to select 160 footmen in the Bailiwick of Lythe and the Moor of Aldeston, and bring them to Carlisle on the Monday next after February 20th (Pat. Rot. 35, Ed. I., Mem. 32).

C

(c) It is also worthy of notice that even when the Scotch were quiet the men of Alston Moor (which, of course, always includes Garrigill) were called upon to support their King by serving under arms.

Edward II. (1307-1327) because of numerous other troubles, was obliged to conclude a truce with Scotland towards the close of his dishonoured reign.

Notwithstanding the quieter times in the north, in 1326 (in the 19th year of Edward II.) Thomas de Featerstanhalgh was appointed to array all the fencible men of . . . the Barony of Tynedale and the Moor of Aldeston to assess them to arms, and to lead them at the King's will, or elsewhere, as shall seem to the said Thomas to be most to the King's advantage, with power to punish any found rebellious in this behalf (vide Pat Rot. 19 Ed. II., Pars. ii., Mem. 12).

3. Passing from the sterner realities of war to the strifes of social and civil life I will mention an episode which

relates entirely to Garrigill. It refers to the year 1288, and concerns one William, who was son of Hugh de Driburn. Driburn is a cluster of dwellings lying on the Rotherhope road, and takes its name from a burn which only runs after excessive storms or the melting of the snow. To-day not more than two families live there, but less than a century ago when the mines were more active, there were nearly 50 "dwellers" at this hamlet. Well, here lived William, the son of Hugh. In the village there was one Patrick the son of a certain Ralph. We cannot give the surnames, for in those days people did not always use them. By some misadventure William of Driburn slew Patrick of the village, and was imprisoned at Alston under charge of murder.

Where was the prison at Alston?

I have found several cases of men breaking out of the Alston prison—not recently—I am speaking of 600 years ago.

But let me go on with the story.

The King learned that William slew Patrick* "by mischance, and not by felony or malice aforethough."

An order was accordingly issued that Thomas de Norman Ville, keeper of the liberty of "Aldenestun," shall deliver William in bail to twelve men, "who shall mainpern to have him before the justices at the first Assize" (Claus. Rot. 16, Ed. I. Mem. 8).

What side-lights are thrown on the life of our village in the "long ago" by such a story as this!

---

* We read of another "Patrick at The Gate" in 1290.

CHAPTER IV.

HOW THE FAITH CAME—RESIDENT CURATE—RULED FROM THE EAST.

It is not possible now to trace the origin of Christianity in this valley.

1. THE DISTRICT.—We have referred to the legend that St. Augustine of Canterbury, who died in A.D. 605, visited Crossfell.

The tradition is utterly worthless. St. Augustine never travelled so far north.

The Apostle of Cumbria was St. Ninian, who died in 432—a son of the ancient Celtic Church, whose See was Candida Casa (Whithorn) in Galloway. Geoffrey Gaimer, *Lestorie de Engles** tells us that even the Picts of Westmoreland were evangelized by St Ninian. He says:

> " Ninan aveit ainz baptize
> Les altres Pictes del regne ;
> Co sunt Les Westmaringiens,

---

* Ed. Rec Com Vol. II., p. 29 L. 967.

Ki donc esteint Pictiens.
A Wyternen gist Saint Dinan
Long tens vint devant Columban."*

There is every probability that his successors would visit the fair-haired Saxon and his retainers, who had settled at the fountain-head of the great River Tyne. Nor do we venture anything when we say that it is more than likely that St. Aidan (635—651), the greatest missionary of northern England, was much more likely to visit the region of Cross Fell than St. Augustine.

But, whatever darkness surrounds the *personnel* of the mission to the Pagan settlers of Garrigill, there can be no doubt as to the fact of the introduction of Christianity into this region in Anglo-Saxon days.

From the manner in which local Church matters are brought before us—

---

* Translation :—Ninian had formerly baptised the other Picts of the kingdom, these are the Westmaringiens who then were Picts.   At Whitherne lies St. Ninian. He came long before Columba.

not as initial, but as fully-established matters—in early Norman days it is clear that Church life and work had been in progress for a considerable period before the Norman advent.

It is well to remember also that the Bishopric of Hexham was created by Archbishop Theodore (668—690), to whom the English Church owes more perhaps than to any other single man. The first Bishop of this See made his accession in 678, and the Diocese was absorbed into that of Lindisfarne in 821. It is not possible to conceive that during that century and a half, with such Bishops at Hexham as John of Beverley, and Wilfrid the missionary who won distant Sussex to The Faith, no effort was made to traverse Whitfield Moor to preach the Gospel to the inhabitants of the South Tyne Valley.

2. ALSTON PARISH.—We know the Church was built in Alston in 1154, for in that year, as related by Hodgson, Henry II. (1154-1189), as patron, presented "his

clerk Galfrid" to the benefice.*

I find two other very early presentations to this benefice.

On December 20, 1292, Hugh, son of Elias de Brengewenne, clerk, was presented (Pat. Rot. 21, Ed. I., Mem. 23).

On April 21, 1304, John de Hauecle was presented (Pat. Rot 32, Ed. I, Mem. 19).

3. GARRIGILL CHAPELRY.—At this time Garrigill also owned its Church or Chapel traditionally dedicated to St. John, Apostle and Evangelist. It has been argued that Garrigill village is older even than Alston, and probably that Garrigill Church was built first. Alston, it has been said, grew up at the junction of the two tracks, formed by the lead carriers, from Nenthead and Garrigill.

Reference has been made to Ivo de Veteri Ponte as a benefactor of the Church. He gave the advowson of the

---

* Hodgson, Northumberland, Vol. iii, pt. 2., p. 36.

Church of "Aldeneston and *the Chapel at Gerardegile*" to the Canons at Hexham Abbey. This was as early as 1215.

He also gave the district of Priorsdale in Garrigill (some 8,000 acres) to the Prior of Hexham.*

The advowson of the Church was recovered from the Prior, but it was restored in 1306, when the King (Edward I.) was lying ill in the winter-time at Lanercost Abbey.†

The possession of Priorsdale by the Abbey remained inviolate until the Reformation.

4. RELATION OF PARISH AND CHAPELRY. The origin of the Chapelry as a separate (quasi) organization from the parish is a very obscure point.

Probably people in outlying parts of a parish would petition for a resident priest, not being satisfied with the

---

* Vide Preface p xv.
† Vide Hexham (Surtees) ii , 119. Rot Cart 34, Ed. I.

occasional services of the clergy of the Parish Church, or the occasional visits of some brother from a neighbouring monastery. In order to obtain their request they would perhaps offer to undertake the maintenance of a resident priest. In such circumstances mutual arrangements could easily be effected without violence to parish interests, or the rights of a Patron.

Some such arrangement was effected very early in the history of Garrigill.

Some time in the XIV. Century the inhabitants of Garrigill made complaint that Sir H———, the chaplain at " Aldeniston, had neglected them, the result being that they claimed to have their own priest living among them.*

The statement by the Rev. W. Nall (Handbook to Alston, p. 81) that the Chapelry was not made a quasi-charge till 1851, is very misleading.†

---

* Hodgson Northumberland, Vol. ii , pt 2, pp. 41-42.
† Vide Ch. vi. The Clergy.

5. THE DIOCESE.—Garrigill is in the county of Cumberland.

But a glance at the map will show that Alston belongs geographically to the eastern side of the country, and not the western. The parish is divided from the rest of Cumberland by a huge barrier of high hills, rising over 2000 feet. But towards the east there is no such dividing line. Alston. by the configuration of the country, is part of Northumberland.

We would naturally expect that Alston Parish, being part of the County of Cumberland, would be in the Diocese of Carlisle (founded 1133), but this is not so. It never was in the Diocese of Carlisle. There is no good reason to doubt that this area was first subject ecclestiastically to Hexham (678), then to Holy Island (821), then to Chester-le-Street (899), and then to Durham (995).

For hundreds of years Alston parochially was in the Diocese of Durham, and is now part of the new Diocese of Newcastle-upon-Tyne. The *Valor Ecclesias-*

ticus of Pope Nicholaus IV., 1291, shews that Alston was then in Durham Diocese. But in the following year, 1292, it was declared upon a perambulation, made by certain Justices Itinerant, and others, that "*the moor and waste of Aldeneston*" were wholly within Cumberland.

The reason for this has been very fully discussed by Chancellor Ferguson in a paper entitled *Why Alston is in the Diocese of Durham and the County of Cumberland.* His statement of the case must be regarded as final.* The reason for the district being taken into Cumberland is a fiscal and financial one. The profits and dues from the mines of Alston Moor were, from the most ancient times, collected for the Crown through the Sheriff of Cumberland at Carlisle, as the head of the lead-mining industry in the North. In this way the Parish became part of the County of Cumberland.

---

* Wallace in his *Alston Moor* (pp 18-21) challenges this theory and elaborates his objection more fully in his MS notes. But his reasoning is utterly futile. I discuss the matter so far as it refers to Garrigill in Chapter XIV.

GARRIGILL CHURCH

IN 1888.

Opp. p. 29.

CHAPTER V

THE CHURCH : DATE OF ERECTION NOT KNOWN—A GALLERY—A CHURCH RATE—VARIOUS REPAIRS.

It is generally stated that the present Church was built in 1790.* But there is no evidence of this among the Church-wardens' papers, nor in the account books of the Chapelry. All available evidence is contrary to this tradition.

I find a remarkable resolution passed at a general meeting of the inhabitants respecting the erection of a Gallery in the Church in 1752.† It is highly improbable that such a heavy expenditure would be incurred in connection with a building which could only stand for another forty years. Further, when the Church was restored in 1890 by the Rev. P. T. Lee, then Curate-in-charge, a huge

---

* This statement appears for instance in *Alston Moor* by William Wallace, p. 64.

† Vide p. 163. Repairs also in 1746.

unsightly Gallery was the conspicious feature of the interior of the Church, doubtless the one erected in 1752.

The resolution to which reference has been made reads as follows :—

"WHEREAS of late by the number of people which resorted to attend divine Service, the Church in Garrigill hath been much crowded and thronged, it was thought by the Churchwardens and others iu the Said Parish very proper to erect a gallery whereby theie might be more room and convenience for the Inhabitants, and others which might resort thither, and to lay the charge of the said gallery upon the land-owners, at whose charge the Church hath always been upheld. Each tenement, whether great or small, paying an equal rate, so that the occupiers of the said tenements may have an equal right or privilege. Therefore it was agreed that the seats or pews upou the said gallery should be numbered according to the number of tenements, and as many ticketts to be drawn for the same, that each might have their lot according to the ticket which hath been drawn by most or all, the seats or pews being in manner following. The seats along the sides of the Church having three tenements joined to a pew or seat, the seats on the end of the said Church, two tenements joined to a pew or seat. And for pieventing any mutiny or disagreement which may happen at any time hereafter, in or about the same, we have annexed a list to be kept as a record in which each pew tenement hath its proper right.

Done in the year of our Lord 1752.
(Signed) JOSEPH WINSKILL, Churchwarden."

The seats were arranged as follows :—

In the first pew : Mr. Crozier, Upper Esh-gill, Tynehead, west side of Tyne.

2nd—Low Redwing, High Rotherhope, Low Roderhope.

3rd.—Crossgill, Low Houses, Garrigill Gate Foot.

4th—Low Howburn, The Whole,* Upper Dodberry.

5th—High Crossgill, Upper Cragg, Garri-gill Gate Head.

6th—Dryburn.

7th—Upper Eshgill Side High Redwing, Shield Hill.

8th—Silly Whole.*

9th—Low Eshgill Side, Hiving.†

10th—Middle Houses and Skides.

11th—Nest.

12th—Low Cragg and Upper Dryburn.

13th—Low Lea House.

14th—Low Eshgill and Garrigill Gate.

15th—Upper Lea House and Turnings.

16th—Middle Cragg and Slaggyburn.

---

* Hole. † Ivy House.

To the pews there were attached metal labels indicating how each pew was appropriated. Their appearance was something like this :—

Six years later a Church Rate was levied for further repairs, but the whole outlay was only four guineas.

CUMBERLAND TO WIT,

A rate and ass'ment made the 12th Day of May, 1758, on the inhabitants of the Chapelry of Garrigill, in the County aforesaid towards the necessary repairs and other charges of the Church of Garrigill for the last year ·—

	£	s	d
John White	0	3	6
John Parmley ... · · ...	0	3	6
Joseph Walton ... · ·	0	3	6
Richard Bell	0	3	6
Joseph Teasdale	0	3	6
Jonathan and Edmond Parmley ...	0	3	6
Christopher Vickers	0	3	6
Robert Brumwill and Party	0	3	6
Mary Cleminson	0	3	6
William Dobson	0	3	6

Thos. Vipond ...	...	...	0	3	6
James Bell	...	...	...	0	3	6
Mr. Smith ...	...	...	0	3	6
Joseph Emmerson ...	...	...	0	3	6
Thos Vipond, Gate Foot ...	...	0	3	6
Robert Bland	...	...	...	0	3	6
Joseph Watson	...	...	0	3	6
John Dickinson and Party	...	...	0	3	6
W. Evans Emmerson ...	...	0	3	6
Joseph Tolson	...	...	...	0	3	6
Robt. Stagg and Dickinson	...	0	3	6
Willm. Walton and Wilkinson ...	...	0	3	6
Jane Wilkinson	...	...	0	3	6
Joseph Low and Little	...	...	0	3	6

Total   £4 4 0

There is a curious entry in 1763 and another in 1766, in the Churchwardens' accounts :—

" 1763. John Madalin repairing Steple £0 1s. 6d."

Had Garrigill Church a steeple at that time ?

" 1766. Repairing the Quire door, and materials £0 1s. 0d."

Does this mean that there was a chancel at this date ?

D

There can be little doubt that "Steple" refers to the bell-cot, and the word "Quire" signifies nothing more than the old "singers' pew."

If the Church were built about 1790, as stated by Wallace, it very soon required attention, for in 1793 these two items appear :—

"Jos. Oyston for repairing Church £4 3s od.

"Wm. Dowson for repairing Church £3 os od.

In 1820, the Church windows were painted, and a new one put in at a cost of £1 7s. 11d. Small sums appear yearly for such items as "new lock," "repairing gate," for "macen work," and very frequently for "walling churchyard wall."

In 1846 there were very considerable sums spent upon the building amounting to about £80. The chief items of expense being Mr. Haldon for joiner's work, £24 18s. 3d. ; painting, etc., £16 3s. 3d. ; H. V. Wilson for wood, £17 9s. od. A stove pipe, metal pegs, cushions, white-washing and labour make up the balance. The largest subscribers were Greenwich Hospital, £13. Messrs. Governor and Company, £10. Mr. and Mrs. Tydell, £15. The collection at the re-opening after sermons by Rev. H. Salvin, Vicar of Alston, and Rev. Joseph Hudson, Curate of Garrigill, brought in £4 5s. 4d.

When the Rev. P. T. Lee entered upon his work here in 1888 the Church was a poor barn-like structure, though the walls were substantial and sound. Its appearance has been fortunately preserved in a sketch by the late Mr. Charles Hicks who was the Diocesan Architect at this time.

Portions of the foundations of a former Church still remain underground on the south side of the present building.

CHAPTER VI.

THE CLERGY.

Garrigill has been a quasi-charge for several centuries. Sometimes the Vicar of Alston was also Curate of Garrigill. More often the Assistant-Curate of Alston held the Garrigill appointment. In 1851 a Parsonage was built. Prior to this, another house was used as The Parsonage. The Rev. Blythe Hurst (1842-1845) resided in Garrigill, occupying Crossgill House.

Several attempts have been made to present a list of the Curates-in-charge. Such lists may be seen in the topographical works of Hutchinson (1778), Hodgson (1827), Jefferson (1840), and in Randal's *State of the Church under the Archdeaconry of Northumberland, and in Hexham Peculiar Jurisdiction* (1779).

The following list, compiled from these authors and the Registers at Garrigill and Alston, is the most complete which has yet been prepared:—

? —Sir ·H——— (Vide p. 26).

? —John de Cokedon.

1422—William Lambert.

1422—Robert Hilton.

> This year Henry V. died (1413—1422).

? —Robert Stehynson.

1495—John Ellison.

1499—Thomas Grey.

1517—D. Stephaneson.

1536—John Hymners.

> This was the year of "The Pilgrimage of Grace."

1558—Henry Yaites.

> This year Queen Elizabeth ascended the Throne

1577—Anthony Watson.

> Vicar of Alston and Curate of Garrigill.

1578—John Hodgson.

1579—1585—John Stephenson.

1604—Herkinwold Seperd.

> *Hampton Court Conference* held at this time.

1618—John Nelson.

1624—R. Young.

1625—F. Hill

> Vicar of Alston and Curate of Garrigill
> The period of The Civil War and Commonwealth.

1661—John Letratus.

---

*See Appendix A.

1665—John Lee.
> The year of The great Plague of London.

? —John Till.

1683—William Stebert.

1696—Nich. Walton.

1728—John Topping.

1731—Daniel Hudson.
> Vicar of Alston and Curate of Garrigill.

1736—Thomas Birkott.

1742—Chris. Gardner.ˑˑ

1754—1790—Thomas Lancaster.†

1790—1833—Benjamin Jackson, Vicar of Alston, acted as Curate. The following appear as assisting him at various times:—

1 —Thomas Winder, 1785—1790.

2.—Thomas Kirby, who signs himself *Curatus pro tempore,* 1791—1820.

3.—Joseph Thompson who continues from 1794 to 1798.

4.—George Dawson, 1791—1807.
The dates of Thos. Kirby, Jos Thompson and Geo. Dawson overlap.

5.—W. H Leech, 1820.
> These five were apparently Curates of Alston.

---

* Signs Wardens' Accounts this year.

† Thomas Lancaster was Curate of Garrigill from 1754 to 1756, and Vicar of Alston from 1756 to 1790. During the latter period he acted as Curate of Garrigill also As Curate of Garrigill he received £20 His licence to Garrigill is among the Alston papers.

1821—1822—Robert Wood.

1822—1826—Thomas Jackson.

1826—John Kirby.

1827—1833—Edward Bigland.*

1834 †—1836—H. T. C. Hine.

1836—? For some time the duty was taken by Thomas Foster, Vicar of Alston.

1839—1841—George Fleming.

1841—James Steele.

1841—1842—Octavius James.

1842—1845—Blythe Hurst.

1845—1847—Joseph Hudson.

1848—1851—John Burton.

1851—1876—George Monkhouse.

1876—James Welsh.

1877—1880—W. Muskett.

1880—1887—The Vicar of Nenthead acted as Curate of Garrigill.

1888—1895—P. T. Lee.

1895—1899—S. H. Greenway.

1899—1901—Cæsar Caine.

1901—1906—Herbert Satchell.

1906—T. Westgarth.

---

* Edward Bigland became Rector of Kirkhaugh.

† In 1834 we have Thomas Harrison " Officiating Minister."

This list cannot be regarded as final, and it is more than likely that some day another searcher may fill up the gaps.

This list goes back certainly for 500 years.

CHAPTER VII.

RECONSTRUCTION OF THE CHURCH—OPENING—CHURCHYARD EXTENTION—NEW ORGAN—GATES FOR THE CHURCHYARD.

From 1888 to 1901 Church life in Garrigill witnessed a great revival in all its departments and organizations.

This work was initiated by the Rev. Percy T. Lee, and carried on by his successors the Rev. S. H. Greenway, and myself.

Mr. Lee has kindly sent me the following account of the period during which he ministered here :—

"When I first saw the old Garrigill Church I questioned whether anywhere in the land there remained such a desolate looking House of God; and yet, when I recall it to mind now, it is not of its imperfections I think. It is not the decrepit harmonium that I remember, but Joe who worked her and humoured her, and got such music out of her as few organists could, and the brave choir who sung to her. It is not of the old cracked stove, giving out more smoke than heat, that I think, but of old Shield who grumbled over it, rattled it, and complained about it. He who had been brakesmen and stoker of one of the first locomotives, and died the last of the old Parish Clerks! The picture of the bare sordid building is brightened to my mind's eye by the figures of John Blacklock, James Vipond, Henry Millican, James Moffat, and a score of others who had not yet, thank God, joined the majority. A Church is not only wood and stone, and of the flesh and blood which entered into the old Garrigill Church I am proud to remember I gained the title—'Yanovoorsels."*

Although it was my first Church it

---

* One of ourselves.

was hard to be proud of it on the first Sunday I saw it.

Let me recall its appearance.

Of packing-case shape; with comparatively low white-washed ceiling; oppressed with an unsightly west gallery; the east wall was broken by a small sized sash window; three sash windows of larger size broke the south wall; while the door and two windows, similar to the east window, looked out to the west; the expanse of the north wall was unbroken save by the fantastic designs drawn by the damp on the one time white plaster.

From the door to the east window ran a narrow aisle in which two persons could barely walk abreast. On either side were narrow pews or pens bearing the names of each homestead in the Chapelry. These terminated two yards from the east wall leaving a narrow space as The Parson's Preserve. The front two pews on the right side were knocked into one to make the singing pew; the front two on the left were similarly treated to hold the

corpse and mourners at funerals, and coal
at ordinary times.   The centre pew on
the same side was half cut away in order
to make room for a small stove, the pipe
from which ran up to the middle of the
ceiling.   The Parson's Preserve was curious.
Two yards wide it extended from wall to
wall.   First on the north was the Vestry,
two yards square.   Next came a three-
decker Pulpit, cut down to one storey.
By the side of this was the bowl of an
ancient font standing on a brick pedestal.
Facing the aisle, under the east window,
was a small table in front of which was
room for only two Communicants to kneel.
On the south side of the altar were two
reading desks facing the congregation and
the Parson's pew.

The want of repair of this edifice
can be gauged by the fact that I counted
seventy rain stains on the ceiling my first
wet Sunday.

The Architect's first plan of restoration was to turn the packing-case into a
nave, build out a chancel on the east

side, with an organ chamber and vestry on the north, a small transept to balance it on the south, with a porch baptistry and bell tower on the west. The estimated cost of this design was £1000. But, alas! when the tenders came in, owing to the cost of building material in such a situation, the lowest reached a sum of £2,300. This sum was far beyond our means, and, after much anxious thought, we determined to follow out to a certain extent the original design, but to apply it in a different manner. We took the east half of the packing-case for our chancel, throwing an arch over from the north to the south wall, raising the floor and leaving the vestry, organ chamber and transept to be built at some future date. The western half of the packing-case was used to commence the nave, the intention being to ultimately pull down the west wall and extend the Church in that direction, building baptistry porch and bell tower on the new end. The extention has, however, never been made, the nave, therefore, retains a curious disproportionate appearance. New ecclesiastical windows were placed in the east and south walls, the building was re-roofed and ceiled with wood, a heating-chamber was excavated below the floor and the seating accommodation and fittings made comfortable and seemly, thus exhausting the thousand pounds we had raised for our first restoration, and accomplishing part, at any rate, of our original design." *

On Friday, July 25, 1890, the Lord Bishop of Newcastle visited Garrigill to re-open the Church and hold a Confirmation.

The first part of the Service was taken by the Rev. A. Baldwin, of Alston, the second part by Canon Cruddas, Rural Dean, the Bishop himself taking the special re-opening prayers. Dr Rutherford, Vicar of Alston, read the Lesson. After an anthem by the Choir, and a collection for the Restoration Fund, which

---

* The old font was placed in the Chancel, and a font for regular use was brought from Alston.

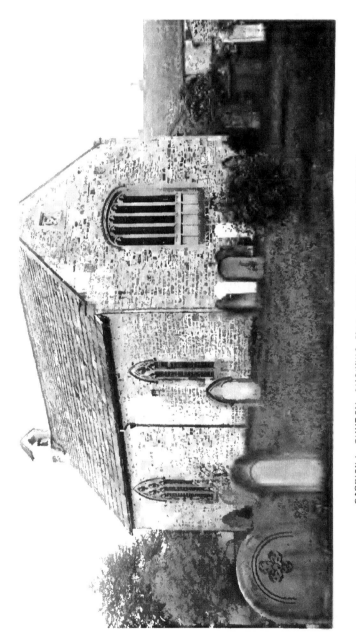

GARRIGILL CHURCH, SHOWING THE SOUTH AND EAST WINDOWS.

Opp. p. 47.

realized £10 3s. 6d. the Bishop held the Confirmation, during which he delivered two Addresses. The following Clergymen were also present : Reverend Canon Dixon, of Warkworth ; Rev. C. Berry, of Nenthead ; Rev. J. T. Anderton, of Knarsdale ; Rev. A. Vaughan, of Lambley ; and the Rev. P. T. Lee, of Garrigill.

The Re-opening Services were continued on Sunday, July 27th, when the Rev. S. Falle, Vicar of Brampton, preached to crowded congregations. The building contained about 250 persons at the Evening Service, the collections on this day bringing in £2 16s. 3d.

In 1893 the necessity arose to enlarge the Churchyard. The Separatist section of the inhabitants resolved upon a Cemetery, and carried their project. This however was not allowed to interfere with the Churchyard enlargement.*

Before long an Organ was added to the Church, being opened free of debt on

* See Chapter XIV.

Sunday, March the 30th, 1894. In September the same year New Oak Gates were added to the Churchyard, a donation from Captain Rose's shooting party.

CHAPTER VIII.

THE WEST WINDOW—THE PORCH— THE CHURCHYARD—THE PARSON- AGE—STABLING—THE CHURCH HOUSE—PREFERMENT.

The splendid advance in Church life and work, described in the previous pages, was efficiently continued by the Rev. S. H. Greenway, who went into residence October 10th, 1895.

The new Priest-in-charge resolutely set himself to extend and consolidate the Church work so effectively inaugurated by his predecessor.

The Church was improved by the removal of two cottage sash windows from the West-end, and the insertion of the present handsome Gothic West window.*

---

* Owing to the decrease in the population it was decided not to extend the nave.

An entrance porch was also added which is not only an adornment to the Church, but has proved a great comfort to the congregation. The total cost was about £120.

The Churchyard was then levelled, planted with trees and provided with footpaths. All the money needed for these purposes was obtained by the day the Church was re-opened for Service.

Meanwhile the Parsonage was thoroughly overhauled, and new drains inserted from the house to the river Tyne. The Parishioners then spontaneously erected, near the Parsonage, stabling for two horses, with coach-house and hay-loft. Almost before this was finished a Committee was formed and plans accepted for the erection of a large hall to seat 250 people for Sunday School purposes, Mission Services, Reading Room, and all other meetings connected with the Church. Hitherto a hired cottage was the only structure available for such purposes, and it was altogether inadequate. This new

GARRIGILL CHURCH.

SHEWING WEST WINDOW AND PORCH.

Opp. p. 50.

building, called the Church House, was opened December, 1898, and about £160 of the cost had been received.

The plans for the Church House, Stables, &c., were prepared by the Rev. S. H. Greenway.

Early in 1899 Mr. Greenway accepted the Vicarage of Felling, and his successful work in Garrigill terminated.

CHAPTER IX.

THE WEATHER VANE—THE VESTRY AND ITS FITTINGS—THE CHURCH HOUSE DEBT—VARIOUS ITEMS.

It is necessary that I shall now refer to the period when I occupied Garrigill Parsonage.

During my incumbency the principal repairs and additions to the Church were the erection of the Font,* the renewal of the Weather Vane, the building of the Vestry, and the removal of £170 debt on the Church House.

The Weather Vane had lost two of its large letters, and was so coated with rust that it refused to obey the strongest wind. It had done duty for half a century, and had to be practically re-made. The work was carried out by the local blacksmith, Mr. J. Greenwell.

---

* Vide, Chapter XI.

The Vestry was erected by a New-castle firm, the plans being prepared by Messrs. Hicks and Charlewood. This addition to the Church is splendidly constructed, every stone being laid with care, and is very strongly built *into* the body of the Church, not merely *against* it. The number of large stone "ties" is much in excess of the necessary number.

For the chimney shaft and the insertion of the two sides of the Vestry, the Church wall was ripped open in three large seams. The chimney shaft, it may be useful to note, is lined with fire-proof pipes or cylinders, and is carried under the roof and is wholly independent of the shaft of the heating apparatus.

The memorial stones of the Vestry were laid on the 13th July, 1901. There were to have been four, but two of the ladies who were expected to officiate were unable to be present. Though the corner stones were reduced from four to two, we are thankful to say this did not affect the financial result. The two stones were placed in position by Miss Cowell, and Miss Walton, in behalf of the lady collectors. There were six lady collectors, who collected £10 3s. 6d. in two or three days in the Chapelry. The amounts for the different districts were as follows :—

Mrs Cæsar Caine and Mrs. John Renwick

The Village	£3	15	0
Mrs. Anderson, Tynehead	2	5	6
Miss L. Walton, Rotherhope......................	1	10	0
Miss Armstrong, Ashgill..........................	1	8	0
Miss Fawcett, Alston Road......................	1	5	0
	£10	3	6

These amounts were laid on the stone placed in position by Miss Walton. Miss Cowell, and the other ladies who were to have taken part, contributed £5 each. At the close of the ceremony there was a collection on the site, which realised over £2. Other sums brought the total for the day to £32 4s.

The form of service was arranged by the Lord Bishop of the Diocese, and the utmost care was taken to carry out his Lordship's wishes in every particular.

THE NORTH SIDE OF THE CHURCH, SHOWING THE VESTRY BUILT IN 1901.

Opp. p. 54.

No names appear on the stones, but each bears a distinguishing mark. The one laid by Miss Cowell carries the most sacred emblem in Christian art and symbolism—The Cross. The one placed by Miss Walton has the ancient Chi Rho monogram—the Greek abbreviation of the name "Christ."

A little memento of the event was presented to Miss Cowell and Miss Walton in the form of a new prayer-book.

The attendance was good considering the season. All around us was the sound of the "winning of the hay." Harvest was in full swing, and it was a marvel that the ceremony could be carried out at all. The success of the day was an astonishment to the country side.

The amounts raised for the building of the Vestry were as follows:—

	£	s.	d.
May 31, 1901—Sale of Work	17	18	0
July 13, 1901—Stone-laying, including cheques	32	4	0
Sept 27, 1901—Dedication, including cheques...	19	18	3
Grant—Diocesan Society	25	0	0

Grant—The Admiralty	15	0	0
Grant—The Barrington Fund	10	0	0
Other Contributions	13	14	0
	£133	14	3

The entire cost of the building (Builder, Architect, Carting, Stone, Faculty Fee, Lime, Furniture, Printing, &c.) was under £150.

It was intended that there should be no debt, and about £20 was set aside from a Sale of Work at the previous Christmas when £80 was raised, to provide against *extras* in building the Vestry. At the last moment the Admiralty claimed £5 6s. od. for law expenses on the Church House Scheme, and the Ecclesiastical Commissioners claimed £10 in payment for the Church House site—liabilities of which no one locally knew anything. The result was that the little reserve fund had to be diverted from the Vestry to the Church House scheme in order to secure the deeds of that building. The whole £80 went to the Church Room Fund, and the Vestry was opened with

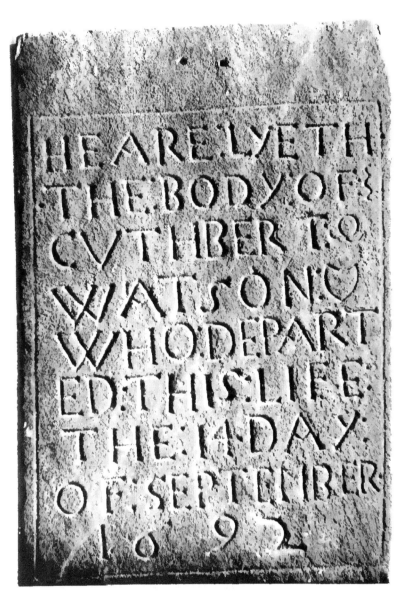

THE TOMBSTONE OF CUTHBERT WATSON IN THE VESTRY.
See Appendix H.

Opp. p. 57.

a small debt of about £15. The Vestry
was built during the last six months of
my residence, and the small balance was
raised after my removal. Two objects of
interest were placed in the vestry :—

(1) The oldest tombstone which I
could discover.

This stone is older than the oldest
local register. The inscription is as follows :
" Heare lyeth the body of Cvthbert
Watson who departed this life the 14th
day of September, 1692."

The small marks used to fill up the
spaces on the stone, as shewn in the
photograph, may have been used by
Cuthbert Watson as sheep marks in his
life time.

(2). I was fortunate in securing at a
sale two mahogany hall chairs which
had been the property of the Rev.
George Monkhouse who was Curate-in-
charge here from 1851 to 1876. These
were put in the Vestry as a memento

of one who spent many of the best days of his life in the interests of both old and young in the Chapelry.

Reference has been made to the Church-House or Sunday School buildings. Upon my going to Garrigill there remained on this building a debt of £170 in all. Such was the untiring energy of the parishioners to remove this debt that I had the happiness to announce its extinction before I left.

CHURCH HOUSE FUND.

Sale, 1899..	£64	0	1
Sale, 1900..	80	14	7
Grant by the S.P.C.K.................................	25	0	0
Advanced by the Treasurer	0	4	6
	£169	19	2

Material for Sewing Meetings, other Goods, Printing, etc , for Sales,.....................	£14	19	0
Repaid Newcastle Diocesan Society,..............	60	0	0
Repaid to the Newcastle Diocesan Society..	20	0	0
Balance paid to Builder.............................	40	1	5
Railings (part of School Scheme)	5	0	0
Ecclesiastical Commissioners for Site.............	10	0	0
Balance paid to Mason	3	12	0
Cupboard.	3	10	0
Balance paid for Seats	2	2	0

Letters and Board for Infants	1	19	0
Books and Cartoons, value £8 from S.P.C.K....	1	15	0
Blacksmith	0	17	2
Law Fees	5	6	0
Old Debt at Bank......................................	0	17	7
	£169	19	2

Several other minor works such as cleaning and colouring the Church, erecting boundary to glebe, etc. involving much expense, were also carried out and paid for.

CHAPTER X.

CHURCH ORNAMENTS AND FITTINGS—THE BELL—OLD PEWTER—PLATE—ALTAR ORNAMENTS—EAGLE LECTERN.

Garrigill Church possesses an excellent bell. Under favourable conditions it has been heard at the most distant parts of Chapelry.

Numerous mis-statements have been current concerning it. I have often seen it stated[*] that it was brought from Dilston Hall in 1716 when James, the third Earl of Derwentwater, was executed for taking part in the Jacobite Rebellion of 1715. Wallace says it "was cast in 1765, or a little after."[†] To put an end to all controversy on the matter I secured,

---

[*] Vide Bulmer, Topography of East Cumberland, 1884.
[†] Wallace : Alston Moor, p 64.

whilst resident in Garrigill, a rubbing of the bell. It bears no inscription except the date 1764.

This date agrees with all we find in the Church books. In the Registers, and Churchwardens' accounts for 1763-4 the history of the bell is very fully displayed.

On the 12th July, 1763, Archdeacon Sharp directed "That the cracked bell be new cast, or changed away, and a bell of the same weight be provided." In the Parish accounts appear these items :—

"1763-4 pd. for new bell £4 3s. 9d."
"Carriage of the bell from Penrith, 1s. 6d."
"Expenses when the bell was hung, 1s. 6d."
"Carriage of the two bells between Alston and Garrigill Gate, 1s. 6d."
The old bell was sold and sent away.

In 1790, Edwd. Raine was paid 1s. for mending bell, and again in 1793, 7s. 10½d. was paid for "repairing bell and bell rope." In 1801, a "bell rope" cost 3s. 10d.

In 1807, Nancy Teasdale, for ringing bell and cleaning churchyard, was paid 7s., and in 1823, James Mulcaster and Ann Spark, for "Tooling Bell," 10s.

Garrigill has several pieces of interesting pewter.*

Anciently the Altar vessels of the Church were in many instances made of pewter. About the beginning of the XIII Century this alloy was condemned for sacred purposes, unless a Church was too poor to purchase silver vessels. Nevertheless, vessels of this material continued to be used down to the beginning of the XIX Century. In some Churches pewter vessels were used on ordinary occasions, whilst the Festivals were marked by the use of vessels of silver.

The Garrigill pieces are :—

1.—A Queen Anne fluted porringer, with two handles, marked G.C.

---

* "Pewder" plates were in common household use in Garrigill in Jacobean times. Wooden trenchers were also used Crockery came into use in the late XVIII Century

QUEEN ANNE FLUTED PORRINGER, FORMERLY USED AS THE EUCHARISTIC CHALICE.

Opp. p. 62.

2.—A pewter basin.

3.—A plate, 11 inches diameter, with moulded edge.

The porringer has, according to tradition, been kept in the Church for fully 200 years.

The basin was formerly kept inside the stone font, and for a time it was used *as* a font, being supported on an iron bracket, attached to a gallery post. Probably this was bought in 1768. It still bears the word "LONDON."

I found the plate was much corroded, and disfigured with a thick coating of varnish. On removing the latter I found knife marks showing it had once done service as a dinner plate. The stamp of one of the London Guilds can still be traced on it. It is now used for collecting in Church.

These articles will become more valuable every year, and the parishioners should see that they are not removed.

I find this in the Churchwardens' accounts:—1759 "Pd. to Hannah Robinson for drisen the lining puder and Church," *i.e.*, dressing the linen, pewter, and Church.

Elsewhere, in the accounts, we read " powther " for pewter.

The Communion vessels belonging to Garrigill consist of an Electro-plate Cup and Paten made by James Dixon and Sons, Sheffield. The Cup is 8 inches high, bell-shaped bowl, gilt inside, with moulded edge. The Paten is 8 inches diameter, with moulded edge 1 inch wide. Both are stamped E.P.B.M.

During the incumbency of the Rev. S. H. Greenway two other vessels were added.

1. A plated Flagon 9½ inches high, by Barnby and Rust of Hull.

2. A Cup, of the same material, and the same makers, 6 inches high.

These were a Thank-offering from Ann Edwards (1898).

GARRIGILL CHURCH.

THE CHANCEL.

Opp. p. 65

The Brass Cross and Eucharistic Lights were presented by the family of the Rev. Octavius James, who was Curate here 1841-2, and are in affectionate remembrance of his work at Garrigill.

The beautiful carved oak Eagle Lectern was the gift of the Shooting Party through Mr. Southby Hewitt in 1900.

F

CHAPTER XI.

CHURCH FURNITURE CONTINUED— THE FONT—OUT OF USE—A PEWTER VESSEL—THE FONT CLEANED—A SECOND FONT—RESTORED— A THIRD STONE.

In the year 1835 the Rev. J. Hodgson, Vicar of Hartburn, visited Garrigill, and saw the Church Font* lying in the Churchyard.

In 1841 the Rev. Octavius James entered upon his duties as Curate-in-Charge, and found the Font still lying as described by Hodgson.

During this period a pewter vessel,† and sometimes an ordinary small basin, was used for Baptisms.

The Clerk at this time was Mr.

---

* Vide p. 52.   † Vide p. 62.

Thomas Peart, to whom the Curate gave instructions to clean up the old Font, with the view of placing it in its proper position within the Church. This worthy project was duly accomplished under the personal supervision of Mr. James.

In 1846, during the incumbency of the Rev. Joseph Hudson, when certain repairs were being executed, the Font was again displaced and put outside the Church door, owing to the expense which would be incurred by having it properly mounted on a stone base. When I lived in Garrigill there was more than one old resident who could remember this second displacement. After a short time it was again put in the Church, and restored to regular use.

Thomas Peart remained Clerk for some years. He was in office when the Rev. George Monkhouse came in 1851, and continued in office for six months afterwards. Mr. Monkhouse received from Mr. James a recital of the vicissitudes of the Font. To me the account was given by Mr. Monkhouse in the form of an affidavit, which I now possess.

Later the Font was superceded by another stone brought from the mother Church, St. Augustine's, Alston, when the whole interior of Garrigill Church was re-modelled during the incumbency of the Rev. P. T. Lee, M.A. (1888-1895). But this time the old stone was not allowed to go outside the building. It was laid in a curtained corner on the south side of the Altar with other things which had fallen into disuse.* This is how matters stood in 1899.

Edward Joicey, Esq., of Blenkinsopp Hall, had offered to pay for the re-erection of the old stone which was shewn to him when he visited the Church. There was also a strong wish on the part of many parishioners that this venerable Font should not be permitted to lie with lumber and rubbish. In this old Font many of the forefathers of the

---

* Vide Note, p. 46.

ANCIENT BOWL

THE FONT: GARRIGILL CHURCH.

Opp. p. 69.

hamlet, who now sleep around their loved house of prayer, were baptized. This fact invested this piece of Church Furniture with associations such as could never attach themselves to the more recently erected Font from Alston. The work was accordingly proceeded with, and a suitable Service to commemorate the occasion was held on October 4th, 1899.

The plans were prepared by Messrs. Hicks and Charlewood, and the work executed by Mr. Richardson of Kirkhaugh.

The Alston Font is still retained, so that the Church now has two Fonts.

One fact about the old Font is a matter for sincere regret. When lying in the Churchyard, from 1835 to 1841, the bowl part below the octagonal upper part of the Font, bore a device in low relief. This disappeared whilst in the hands of Thomas Peart. Any one who examines the Font can detect the skilled mason's chisel marks on the upper squared part, whilst the bowl part is hacked by an unpractised hand. Possibly there was on the stone some ecclesiastical symbolism which offended the Clerk. So the old Font (long may it be treasured) will, unfortunately, go down to posterity injured, and to some extent defaced by the Parish Clerk's meddlesomeness.

Some time ago a villager announced that the Font in the Church was *made* by Thomas Peart, and that the ancient Font was in his own private possession. I made personal application to him to favour me with a view of the relic, but I was promptly refused. Now, *if there be another Font in existence*, none of the foregoing statements are affected. It only proves that Garrigill Church has *three* Fonts, not *two*. I hope the third Font, if genuine, will be returned, by some means, to the Church to which it belongs.

From the description I have heard of this third stone I think it may be a Stoup for Holy Water.

For some further particulars the reader is referred to Appendix B.

CHAPTER XII.

THE CHURCHWARDENS—METHODS OF ELECTION—THEIR DUTIES— LIST—THE CONSTABLES— THE ROADS—VERMIN.

The Church Wardens' papers for the last one hundred and fifty years are nearly complete. They contain such a mass of information that they should be carefully mounted and bound. From a study of these documents the following interesting facts may be gleaned :—

1.—Every landholder was expected to serve in this office.

2.—There were always two wardens, one being chosen from each side of the river. Further, when the selection was going *down* one bank of the stream the rotation was going *up* the other bank. This was the rule but it was often broken.

3.—A century and a half ago the religious bitterness which to-day often forbids a dissenter being interested in his district Church did not exist.* In this matter, alas! there has been a lamentable loosening of the bond of Christian charity.

4.—The duty to serve as warden would come by turn to a woman, or some one not desiring to occupy the post. In these circumstances another person would serve instead. Thus the land opposite a warden's name does not ncessarily indicate his residence, but the holding he represents, his own or another's.

5.—The following were some of the duties of the Churchwardens :—

(1) They collected and spent the Church rate.
(2) Were *ex-officio* Trustees of the Day School Buildings.
(3) Appointed and paid the village constable.
(4) Relieved the poor, and, in particular, soldiers passing through the village.
(5) Superintended the work of the road surveyor.
(6) Exterminated vermin—a price being fixed upon the head of every fox, otter, &c.

---

* The schism at Redwing had become extremely feeble. Vide, Chapter XIX.

6.—Among their privileges were :—

(1) A journey to Newcastle yearly at the expense of the parish for the Visitation.
Usually they spent £5.
(2) A dinner with the principal parishioners at the expense of the patron.

7.—Of the items which refer to fabric repairs some are of special interest. This, for instance, is interesting :—" 12 poke full of Fogg, 2s. od." " Fog " is the local word for " moss."* Moss was used for packing between the flat stones with which the Church is roofed.

The following in 1733 is explanatory : " For getting coals and taking lime out of ye kill and ruddleng it, bringing to ye Chapel and working it, getting Fog and bringing it ready for stopping £1 6s. 6d."

The same practice prevails elsewhere. A Shropshire Vicar wrote in the *Church Times*, March 24, 1905 :—" In this part of the world our roofing used to be done with rough split stones ; part of my house

* The aftermath is also called " fog " or " fog grass."

and my stables are still roofed in this manner. The stones are not as cleanly split as slates are, and consequently snow often blows in. To obviate this the roof is mossed—*i.e.*, moss is packed in between the stones. I have had some mossing to do, and know the value of it."

The use of "fog" in Garrigill district in roof construction is still common.

The twelve "poke" (bags) full of "fogg" could easily be used in repairing so large a roof as that of the Church.

In 1798, we have this item in the Parish Books. "For repairing the Stable belonging the Parish 6s. 9d."

This Stable, used by persons riding to the Services at Church, occupied the S.W. corner of the Churchyard. The site is easily discovered by continuing the line of the south wall westward. I have not been able to discover how the site became alienated.

Before presenting the list of Church-wardens I should state two or three facts.

1.—About the beginning of the XIX. Century the old system of election shows decided signs of breaking down. Some chosen as wardens appear to ignore their election, and their work is of necessity done by others. In this list only those are mentioned who actually performed the duties of the office.

2.—The accounts are made up at all times of the year from January to December though running from Easter to Easter.

3.—The accounts for some years are missing.

These facts show that the compilation of a complete list is impossible.

The list curiously opens with the ancient Norman name of the district, in duplicate :—

1737—John Vipond.
      Thomas Vipond.

1738-9—Thomas Vipond of Skides.
         Thomas Vipond of Dryburn.

1742—John Smith.
       Thomas Brown.

1743—Thomas Watson.
       Richard Wallas.

1745—Joseph Walton.
       Joseph Dickinson.

1746—Joseph Dickinson.
       Joseph Walton

1750—John Vipond

1753—Ralph Watson *
       Christopher Vicars.

1754—John Walton.
       Robert Brommwell.

1755—John Walton.

1756—Robert Brumble.
       John Walton.

1757—William Archer.
       Robert Bland.

1758—William Bateson.
       Isaac Vipond.

1759—Thomas Vipond.
       John Vipond.

1760—Nicholas Vipond, Dryburn.
       William Bateson, Low Houses.

1761—William Bateson, Turnings.
       Thomas Vipond, Skides.

1762—Thomas Pearson, Tynehead.
       John Parmley, Howburn.

---

* A singularly well executed Paper. The account is rendered on 23rd, Aug. 1754, but the expenses are for the year, Easter 1753 to Easter 1754.

1763—John Smith, Bleagate.
     William Hetherington, Tynehead.
1764—None given.
1765—William Hetherington, Hole.
     William White, Howburn.
1765—Joseph Cragg, Hill
     Thomas Walton, Nest.
1766—John Coultard, High Eshgill.
     John Walton, Low Rodrup.
1767—Simon Elliot, Lee House.
     Joseph Lee, Flatt.
1768—John Rhenwick, Low Eshgill.
     John Parmley, Low Rodrup.
1769—John Walton, Silly Hole.
     Joshua Stagg, Low Lee House.
1770—Joseph Teasdale, Little-Gill
     George Emmerson, Esgill-side.
1771—Thos. Holmes, Low Crag.
     John Smith, High Crossgill.
1772—Thomas Hodgson, Low House, Rodrup.
     John Snowdon, Eshgillside.
1773—John Curragh, Low Crossgill.
     Joseph Vipond, Middle Cragg.
1774—William Shield, Snapper Gill.
     John Kindred, Slaggie Burn.
1775—John Walton, High Cragg.
     Robt. Stagg, Gatchead.
1776—Joshua Archer.
     Robt. Bromwell.
1777 *—Isaac Vipond.
     Richd. Dodd.

* John Davidson served this year for one warden.

1778—Joseph Winsgill.
    Thos. Vipond.
1779—Joseph Winskill.
    Thos. Bland.
1780—Isaac Vipond.
    Richard Dodd
1781—John Vipond.
    George Ramsay.
1782—Thomas Vipond.
    George Ramsay.
1783—Thomas Watson.
    John Watson.
1784—Jos. Hetherington.
    Utrick Walton.
1785—John Kindred.
    Thomas Smith.
1786—Robert Lancaster.
    Jos. Watson.
1787—Thomas Kidd.
    John Kindred.
.1788—Simon Elliot.
    Wm. Todd.
1789—William Currah.
    John White.
1790—Thomas Vipond.
    John Watson.
1791—Robert Bell.
    Thomas White
1792—Jacob Ritson
    Anthony Martindale
1793—Anthony Martindale.
    John Edger.
1794—John Edger
    Thomas Watson.

1795—John Curragh.
 John Parmley.
1796—Joseph Watson.
 Cudbert Hetherington.
1797—John Kindred.
 Thomas Pearson.
1798—Ralph Vipond.
 John Kindred.
1799—Ralph Vipond.
 John Kindred.
1800—Ralph Vipond.
 John Kindred.
1801—John Kindred.
 John Johnstone.
1802—Thomas Shaw.
 John Johnstone.
1803-4—Samuel Hudspith.
 Thomas Vipond.
1804-5—Samuel Hudspith.
 Thomas Vipond.
1805-6—Samuel Hudspith.
 Jonathan Woodmas.
1806-7—Isaac Hall.
 Thomas Watson.
1807-8—Jno. Vipond, Low Redwing.
 James Dickinson, Eshgillside.
1808-9—Crislefer Walton, Low Eshgill.
 Thomas Smith, Tynehead.
1809-10—John Curragh, High Eshgill
 Thomas Smith, High Lee House.
1810-1—Edward Coats, Whole. *(sic)*
 Thomas Walton, Low Lee House.
1811-2—Thomas Kidd, Tynehead.
 Richard Lowthian, High Crossgill.

1813—John Slack, Townmeadow heads.
John Curragh, Crossgill.

1814—John Slack, Nest.
John Bradwell, Gate.

1815—John Slack, Bleagate.
Thomas Brown, Hivin

1816—John Slack, Flat
Ralph Vipond, High Gate Foot

1817—John Slack, High and Low Silly Hole.
Ralph Vipond, Low Gate Foot.

1818—John Slack, Low Craig.
Thomas Peart, Turnens.*

1819—John Fairlamb, Middlecrag
Thomas Watson, High Redwing

1820—Thomas Watson, Skides.
Thomas Hetherington,

1821—John Vipond, Redwing.
John Wallace, Fewsteads.

1822—Thomas Vipond, Dryburn.
Thomas Shaw, Shield Hill.

1823—Joseph Pearson, Middle Houses.
Joseph Watson, Dryburn.

1824—Joseph Pearson, Lowhouses.
Joseph Watson, High Roderhope.

1825—Christopher Moffat, Slaggyburn.
Joseph Hall, Windy Hall.

1826—Thomas Wailes, Little Gill, Lowhouse.
William Coats, Doddberry and Beldy.

1827—Joseph Varty as substitute for Thos. Taylor of
Bunkers Hill, and William Bainbridge, and
John Scott, for Loninghead, being one tene-
ment; William Coats for Robert Hodgson,
Esq , for Little Gill Tenement.

---

* Turnings.

1827-8 * —Thomas Vipond, Low Rodderup.
    Joseph Renwick, Lower Eshgillside.

1828-9—Emerson Dickinson, Heigh Esbgillside.
    Joseph Renwick, Tynehead.

1830—Anthony Siddel, Low Eshgill.
    Joseph Renwick, Heigh Lee House.

1830-1—John Currah, Heigh Eshgill.
    Joseph Renwick, Howgill Sike.

1831-2—William Coats, Hole.
    Joseph Renwick, Heigh Crossgill.

1832-3—Wm. Coats, for Joseph and John, Hospitel Tene-
    ments, Tynehead, and
    Joseph Renwick, for Isabella Watson, Low Crossgill.

1833-4—John Hodgson, Town Meadow Heads
    Joseph Renwick, Gatehead.

1834-5—John Brown, Ivy Tenement.
    John Hodgson, Nest

1835-6—George Peart, Garrigill Gate Foot.
    John Teasdale, Bleagate.

1836-7—James Vipond, Garrigill Gate Foot.
    Adam Bell, Flatt.

1838—Thos. Holm, † Turnings.
    Adam Bell, Silly Hole.

1839—Thos. Holm, Redwing.
    Robt. Davidson, Nether Crag.

1840—John Watson, Skides.
    Thos Holmes, Middle Crag.

1841—Thomas Holmes, High Crag.
    Joseph Watson, Dryburn.

---

* There is a little confusion at this point There are
two sets of Wardens apparently for the same year.
   † Holmes (?)

G

1842—Joseph Watson, High Rotherhope
    Thomas Holmes, Fewsteads.

1842-3—Isaac Vipond, Dryburn.
    Thomas Holmes, Shield Hill.

1843-4—Thomas Spark, Slaggyburn.
    George Swindle, Middlehouses.

1844-5—John Watson, Lowhouses.
    Wm. Wallace, Lowhouses

1845-6—Stephen Hodgson, Littlegill.
    Thomas Watson, Dodberry.

1846-7—Hugh Spark, Loaning Head.
    Thomas Parmley, Low Rotherhope.

1847-8—Jason Stephenson.
    Thomas Parmley.

1848-9—John Young, Howburn.
    Joseph Renwick, Nether Eshgill Side.

1849-50—Jos Pearson Slack, High Lee House
    Thomas Slack, Upper Eshgill Side.

1849-50—Thomas Slack, Ashgill, and John Millican,
    junior, for Joseph Slack and John Millican,
    High and Middle Lee House.

1850-1—Thomas Slack, Ashgill, and John Watson, Low
    Lee House, and Howgill Syke.

1851-2—Thomas Slack, Ashgill, and Joshua Mulcaster,
    High Crossgill.

1852-3—William Gill, Low Crossgill, and Joseph Vipond,
    Tynehead.

1853-4—Edward Raine, Gate Head, and William Gill,
    The Hole

1854-5—William Bird, Ivy House, and John Hodgson,
    Side Head, Tenement

1855-6—William Bird, Gate Foot, and John Hodgson,
    Nest.

1856-7—James Vipond, and John Cousin, for Gate Foot Tenement, and John Hodgson, Low Cow Gap.

1857-8—James Vipond, Turnings, and John Hetherington, The Flat.*

1858-9—Matthew Bramwell, Redwing, and John Hetherington, Silly Hall (*sic* for Hole).

1859-60—Matthew Bramwell, Skydes, and William Blair, Low Craig.

1860-1—Joseph Smith, Middle Craig, and John Watson of Dryburn

1861-2—John Vipond, Dryburn, and Joseph Smith, standing for Fewsteads.

1862-3—John Watson, for High Rotherhope, and Robert Richardson, for Fewsteads.

1863-4—Isaac Varty, Slaggyburn, and Thomas Shaw, Shield Hill.

1864-5—Friend Herdman, Middle Houses, and Hugh Kearton, Low Houses.

1865-6—Joseph Smith, Low Houses, and William Hodgson, Little Gill.

1866-7—Milburn Parmley, Low Rotherhope, and Isaac Craig, Force Green.

1867-8—Henry Walton, How Burn, and Jonathan Carr, Bunker's Hill

1868-9—George Pickering. Lane Head, and Robert Dent deputy for Matthew Henderson for the Hole.

1869-70—John Hodgson, Side House, and Thomas Archer, Windy Hall

1870-1—Joseph Renwick, Ashgill Side, and Joseph Renwick for Tynehead.

---

* Joseph Coulthard had been appointed but did not act.

1871-2—Thomas Bell, Lee House, and John Hetherington, Ashgill Side

1872-3—John Siddle, Low Ashgill, and John Wilkinson, Low Lee House.

1873-4—Isaac Curragh, West Ashgill, and John Slack, Middle Crossgill.

1874-5—George Pickering, Tyne House, and Robert Dent, Crossgill.

1875 6—Henry Millican, Gate Head, and Robert Dent, The Hole.

1876-7—William B. Brown, Ivy House, and Thomas Richardson, Nest.

1877-8—John Hetherington, Gate Foot, and Jacob Smith for Cow Gap.

1878-9—Joseph Renwick.

1879-80—Matthew Bramwell.*

1880-1—William Ward, Skydes, and Thomas Pickering, Silly Hole.

1881-2—Peter Vipond, Dryburn, and John Davidson Craig.

1882-3—John Watson, High Rodderup, and John Bell Craig.

1883-4—Joseph Varty, Rodderup, and M. Shaw, Shield Hill †

1884-5—Thomas Kearton, and Friend Herdman.

1885-6—H. Jackson, and C. Hardy.

1886-7—H. Jackson, and C. Hardy.

---

* No appointment recorded. M B. fulfilled the duties of the Office.

† The Vestry minutes give no name, but "The occupier of Shield Hill."

In the Vestry meeting, May 6, 1886, the question was raised as to the wisdom of electing by rotation according to Tenements. From this date the old order of election entirely disappears

1887-8—Henry Walton, and Jonathan Carr.

1888-9—Henry Walton, and Julien Bell

1889-90—John Hall, Windy Hall, and John Hodgson, Water Partings.

1890-1—John Hetherington, Snappergill, and Philipson Millican, Tynehead

1891—John Armstrong, Ashgill, and Tom Renwick, Tynehead.

1892—Thomas Richardson, Ashgill, and Tom Renwick, Tynehead.

1893—Thomas Renwick, Ashgill, and Henry Millican, Gatehead.

1894—
1895—
1896— Henry Millican, Gatehead, and Thomas Renwick, Ashgill.
1897—

1898—John Hall, and Nicholson Anderson.

1899—
1900—
1901— Nicholas Anderson, and John Renwick.
1902—
1903—

1904— Thomas Walton, How Burn, and John Hall, Windy Hall.
1905—

It will be interesting to illustrate the duties of the Churchwardens apart from the maintenance of the Church fabric.

I.—An entry in the accounts of the Constable for the year 1805 illustrates the fact that the Constable was responsible to the Wardens:—

"Feb. 14, 1805.

Returned by Hanage Dobson Constable to the present Churchwardents *(sic)* £4 3s. 0d."

This was his balance in hand.

The following is a specimen of a Balance Sheet of the Constable :—

March 7, 1788.

"Isaac Teasdale the Old Constable Made up his Accounts to Jas. Watson present one. The amount of the 'Sess'* is £7 16s o½d.

Paid to Ralph Vipond for ye last year	o	8	6
For Purveys and carring *(sic)* them in	3	o	o

---

* Assessment.

For serving warrents	0	2	0
For warrents and 7 journeys to Penrith	I	15	0
For John Wren for writing ...	0	3	6
For a Travelar upon distress ..	0	2	0
Robert for entering accounts 2 calls	0	2	8
For writing a Millita (sic) List	0	3	0
Isaac Teasdale for taking in names and going about the Parish	0	8	6
	£6	5	2
Jas. Watson received of Isaac Teasdale unexpended ...	I	10	10 "

The following is the list of Constables for the latter part of the XVIII Century :—

1764—John Vipond.
1765—Joseph Wilkinson.
1766—Thomas Dickinson of Leehouse
1767—John Bell.
1768—Jona Wren.
1769—Edward Little.
1770—Thoma* Vipond.
1771—Isaac Vipond.

---

* Sic. Thomas.

1772—Joseph Emmerson.
1773—Thomas Hodgson.
1775—Joseph Teasdale
1776—Thomas White.
1777—George Bromwell, Low Rotheroup.
1779—John Walton
1780—Stephen Hodgson.
1781—Joseph Smith.
1782—John Todd.
1783—John Walton.
1784—William Hunt.
1785—*
1786—Ralph Vipond.
1787—Isaac Teasdale.
1788—James Watson
1789—John Jonstone.
1790—John Wallas.
1791—Jos. Winskiel.
1792—†John Cowper.
1793—Joseph Watson
1794—Joseph Renwick
1795—James Dickinson.
1796—James Dickinson.
   John Spark.
1798—William Hetherington.
1799—William Hetherington.
1800—John Slack.
1801—John Slack.
1802—John Slack.
1803—John Dobson of Aldston.
1804—Hanage Dobson.

---

* In 1785 William Hunt makes up his accounts but no new Constable is named   He continued in office.

† Date has been altered to 1791 in Register.

It appears that soon after this the election of the Constable became the duty of Manor Court sitting at Lowbyer, Alston.

I have taken the following from the Records of the Court :—

"MANOR OF ⎫ The Court Leet and view of Frank-
 ALSTON ⎬ pledge of our Sovereign Lord the
 MOOR ⎭ King with the Court Baron and Customary Court of the Commissioners and Governors of the Royal Hospital for Seamen at Greenwich, in the County of Kent, Lords of the said Manor holden at the Lowbyer in, and for the said Manor, on Friday, the sixteenth day of October 1812; before Henry Dixon, gentleman, steward of the said Court.

"The names of the Jurors :—

Mr John Little		Mr. R. Elliott
„ Teasdale Thompson		„ W. Watson
„ J Vipond, Redwing		„ J. Watson
„ John Shield	sworn	„ J Richardson
„ John Robinson		„ J. Smith
„ William Robson		„ M. Charlton
„ John Parmely		

"Who being sworn and charged, present as follows :—

"We present Thomas Watson of Skides in Garrigill to be Constable for the Township of Garrigill."

The Court presented again in 1820.

Under date of 13th Oct. 1820 we have this :—

" We present Thomas Wailes of Little Gill to be Constable for the township of Garrigill "

II.—The following abstracts from the Wardens' papers refer to the repair and maintenance of the roads.

"Cumberland Leath Ward.

To the Constable of the Division of Garrigile in the Parish of Alston in the said County.

Whereas Complaint and Information on Oath of John Dickinson of Garrigilegate in the Parish and County aforesaid at a private Session held at Penrith for the said ward, hath this Day been made before us, that the several persons whose names are in the shedule hereunder written particularly mentioned, Inhabitants within the said Division of Garrigill in the Parish of Alston aforesaid have severaly made default in perform-ing their statue work or six Days Labour within the said Division, although, duly Sommond to perform the same, by the said John Dickinson, late Surveyor of the Roads within the said Division. We do, therefore, hereby require you imediately to sumon the same several persons that they personaly appear before us, or some other of His Majesty's Justices of the peace for for the said Ward and County on Tuesday, the tenth Day of October next, at the New George in Penrith, at ten in the forenoon, at a Private Session then and there to be held to show cause why they did not perform such statute Labour, and why the penalty for such their default should not be Levyed. Given under our hands and seals this 30th Sept., 1769.

Robert Stagg	Robert Bell
Joshua Stagg	Thomas Harler
Joseph Renwick	John Nattris
Henry Renwick	Jacob Watson
William Renwick	Isaac Cooper
Joseph Renwick	John Salkeld
Henry Renwick	Thomas Salkeld
Joseph Green	Joseph Salkeld
John Nicholson	John Shield
Joseph Cooper	Joseph Shield
Thomas Nixon	John Lee, Bleagate
John Hutchinson	Walton of the Nest
John Wilkinson	Thomas Walton
Thomas Wilkinson	The Rev Mr. Nelson *
Joseph Wilkinson	Richard Renwick
Joseph Clemitson	Joseph Hutchinson "
John Rowe	

At a meeting of landholders of Garrigill, March 31st, 1826, for the taking into consideration the appointment of a person to be Highway Surveyor of the said Chapelry :—

---

* The dissenting preacher at Redwing In Mr. Nelson's time the dissenting congregation dwindled almost to extinction. This was owing to the new enthusiasm of the Methodists who had just arisen.

" Resolution 1st —That it is agreed at this meeting to have a permanent officer of the high-ways with an annual salary of five pounds.

Resolution 2nd.—That the same person who is appointed for the Parish of Alston be chosen for Garrigill.

Resolution 3rd.—That if the said officer fail to give satisfaction at a legal meeting called by the said Chapelry he may be dis-charged by a majority of the said meeting

Thomas Dickinson.	Arthur Hutchinson.
Thomas Shaw.	John Millican.
Adam Elliott.	Thomas Pearson.
Joseph Pearson.	Jon. Watson.
John Vipond	John Pearson.
John Stout	Thomas Greenwell.
Joseph Slack.	John Clementson.
John Slack.	John Elliott.
Henry Wilkinson.	Wm. Coats."

Two years later we have the follow-ing about a road which still awaits the attention of the parish :—

" May 23, 1828.
At a Vestry meeting this Day held pursuant to public notice, it is agreed by a majority of the in-habitants of Garrigill Township that the road leading from Low Houses to Shield Hill Top is not to be repaired by the Parish, that they will suffer an indict-ment.

Thomas Dawson, Thomas Simpson, Joseph Pearson
Slack, Joseph Vipond, John Slack, Wm. Vipond,
Joseph Reuwick, James Vipond, John Coats

III.—There are many references to the
destruction of Vermin such as the following:—

* To Thomas Vipond, of Skidy,
    for a Fowmert * head ...   o o 4
To Joseph Watson, of Weardale,
    for a fox † head   ...   o 5 o

---

* A Polecat.

† ' Peter Lombard ' in *The Church Times* March 24,
1905, has this note:—

" A correspondent sends me from Northumberland
a number of entries from his parish accounts of money
paid for foxes' heads, the rate being 12d for a fox
and 6d. for a cub. I don't know how public opinion stands now in that part of the world, but there
would be fierce indignation in the South over such
payments. John Leech had a picture in *Punch*
once of a clerical-looking party walking with a book,
and two fox hunters are riding past him, one of
whom says, ' Look at that fellow. To my knowledge
he has killed two foxes, and yet he goes about with
a hymn book under his arm.' "

An Essex rector caps this. The governess asks
her pupil, the squire's son, " Why was Adam turned
out of Paradise, Reginald?" "Dunno, miss; perhaps
he shot a fox."

In 1742, one pound two shillings was paid for Foxes and Foul Marts.

In 1747, William Johnston got one shilling for two otter.

This Chapter may be appropriately concluded with a few odds and ends in the way of entries. They are chiefly curiosities in the way of spelling :—

" Carges at Pom Sunday * and Good Frida."

"John Pattison for a Prairbook 5s. 6d."

" Cherge for a shoulger 2 nights by vartue of a pas to parish ofisers, 1s."

" Paid to John Vipond for a new pue and won day repairing seats, 6s."

---

* Palm Sunday was one of the great days of the year. The children were catechised in Church, and a liberal allowance in refreshments was allowed to visitors who came from far and wide.

CHAPTER XIII.

THE REGISTERS—A RESOLUTION— A "KIST"—THE OLDEST REGISTER— REGISTERS AT DURHAM—A COPY— LATIN AND GREEK.

It is pleasing to find that the people of Garrigill understood the value of their Registers and other documents.

This is evidenced by the following :—

"Garrigill Gate,
January 8th, 1813.

At a Vestry Meeting held here this day, pursuant to public notice given, it is unanimously agreed that all the Register Books belonging to Garrigill are to be kept in Garrigill as usual under inspection of the Churchwardens as witness our hands.

John Currah.
Joseph Slack.
Ralph Vipond.
Thomas Brown.
John Whitfield.
George Swindle.
Isaac Vipond.
William Greenwell.
John Vipond.
Joseph Vipond.
Thomas Watson.
Thomas Smith.
James Bell.
Thomas Archer."

From this time the various books and papers were kept in an iron "Kist."*

This "safe" of the Georgian days cost the Chapelry ten pounds.

In the Churchwardens' accounts under date July 18, 1813, we have:

"To an iron Chist, £9 1s. 6d.
For carriage £0 13s. od."

---

* Chest.

This box is still in use.

Parchment was used for the Registers until a late period. In 1754 eleven shillings was paid for a parchment "Redchester."

The oldest Register of Garrigill Chapelry is kept at Alston with the oldest Alston Register, as one book.*

The entries belonging to Garrigill are as follows :—

I. BAPTISMS : 1704—1729.

Here we have a most unique feature. I have not heard of the like in any other parish—"A distinct Register of Nonconformists." This covers the period from 1704—1728. The Nonconformists were (1) the Presbyterians introduced by Burnand of Brampton, or (2) the Independents who followed John Davy, the "preacher" at the house of Reginald Walton at Tynehead.†

---

* There are really two books, for the Garrigill parchment is less than that of Alston.

† See Chapter xix.

II. MARRIAGES: 1699—1730.
III. BURIALS: 1699—1729.

The Garrigill entries are earlier than those of Alston by two years. It is a local tradition that all records prior to 1699 were sent to Durham. I have investigated this matter and find that there are Garrigill Registers at Durham, but the earliest is dated 1760. The earliest parish registers at Durham only date from 1742. Prior to that they were destroyed by fire.

Besides the original Register there is a *copy* very carefully executed. This copy is endorsed :—
" Copy of Register of the Parish of Alston commencing 1st. Sept. 1706 and ending 4th March, 1729. Copied by order of the Rev. Archdeacon Thorpe, A.D. 1811, by me

John Coulthard."

At the end there is a certificate :—
" We, the undersigned, having perused and examined this copy, Do certify it to be

a true and faithful copy of the Register of the Parish of Alston, or as much so as the Defaced State of the Old Books would admit.

Benjn. Jackson,
Vicar of Alston."

The Garrigill section of this Register was published in 1901.

A few notes about the Alston part of this Register may be of service if given here.

The most peculiar fact is that some of the entries are in Latin,* and one is in Greek. These deviations must be put down to the caprice of the Vicar, though it must be said that the good man had a purpose in eschewing English phraseology.

The learned languages are reserved for entries which refer to the Vicarage, and the family of the Schoolmaster.

---

* At this late date the regular use of Latin in Registers had ceased.

Here is a specimen of the Latin entries:—

"Elizabetha Reverendi Vicarij de Alsta: Nicholai Walton ffilia sacro Xtianom Ritu aspersa fuit Decimo Octobris Millesimo Septingentesimo Sexto."

Translation :—

"Elizabeth, the daughter of the Reverend Nicholas Walton, Vicar of Alston, was baptised (by sprinkling), according to the sacred rite of the Christian Church (Christians), on the 10th of October, 1706.

I have commended for beautiful penmanship the copy of this Register, made by John Coulthard, in 1811. But the copyist was ignorant of Latin, and these Latin entries are dreadfully blundered in his copy.

The Greek entry is an attempt at composition, and not a mere use of Greek characters, but one word is mis-spelt and in another a masculine form is used where a feminine ending is required! The writer has also used archaic ligatures.

Here is the entry just as I copied it.

Ριχάρδ℺ Γαλάσσε ὁ Γραμματα:
διδάσκαλ℺ καὶ ἡ Μαρία Λίττλε
ἄλυτ᾽ τῆς ἱερῆς Συξυγίας τῶ
δεσμῶ συνγεμοσσομενοι ·κ· δ·
τῶ Μαΐῶ Α·Ψ·Γ·

Translated, allowing for errors, the entry reads:—

" Richard Wallasse * the Grammar School Master and Maria Little were united to become joint burden bearers in the indissoluble bond of Holy Wedlock on the 24th of May, 1703."

* The writing here has nearly perished, and this word has been read to visitors as Uniacke (an Irish Name), but this is certainly

THE CHURCHYARD—WALLACE'S ACCOUNT—CRITICISM—EARLY BURIALS—ROAD FROM KIRKLAND— CEMETERY—"NORTH SIDE"—CROSS SOCKET.

Wallace states "The old people living in Garrigill frequently said that in former times there was a closer connection between the parish of Garrigill and the parish of Kirkland than with the parish of Alston.

"What this connection consisted in, or how, or when formed, I have never been able to learn with certainty. It is, however, very remarkable that the dead were carried from Garrigill to be interred at Kirkland.

"I was once informed by Mr. Thomas Millican, who was the agent for Messrs. Fydell and Tufnell's, Tynehead Manor, that a corpse was taken from Garrigill, in the depth of winter, to be interred at Kirkland. The funeral party was overtaken with a snow storm, and had to return home to save their lives, leaving the coffin on the top of Cross Fell, where it remained for a fortnight. When the storm subsided they brought the corpse back to Garrigill and buried it in a piece of Glebe Land. The Bishop of Durham having been informed of the circumstance ordered a portion of the Glebe Land to be walled in, and then came to consecrate it for a burial ground. I suppose this occurred about the middle of the seventeenth century or a few years later.

"Mr. Millican informed me that for some years after this event the Registers of Baptisms and Deaths were written on slips of paper and were put through an opening into a box kept at the Fox Inn. The box was occasionally opened by a Clergyman and the Registers sent to Durham.

"This very remarkable circumstance of

the pastoral people at Garrigill burying
their dead in Kirkland Parish may throw
some light on the question why Alston
Moor is in the county of Cumberland. . . .

"It would seem probable that the
Anglo Saxons who formed the fell-side
village communities on the west side of
the Cross Fell range of mountains, took
possession of the fertile land on the banks
of the Tyne river for summerings of their
flocks of sheep and cattle, and that
shepherds resided in *shelis* to attend to
and protect their flocks from wolves until
the autumn.

"A portion of one of the principal
streams in Alston Moor is called Shield
Waters, and a number of the farm houses
are called Shields. The migratory population would be subject to the county
jurisdiction connected with their principal
place of abode. . . . . The desire to be
interred at the place of sepulture of their
fathers is a natural one, and sufficiently
accounts for the practice of the pastoral

people of Garrigill parish to continue burying their dead at Kirkland."[*]

We must regard these paragraphs as the weak part of Wallace's excellent book. Whatever dear old Thomas Millican told him, Wallace writes down, and makes a theory to suit the statements. He makes no attempt to distinguish between local traditions and historic facts.

It is an established fact that the reason why this district is included in Cumberland concerns the *mines*, not, as Wallace suggests, the *cattle*.[†]

If we accept the theory of Mr. Wallace that the Anglo-Saxons who settled in Garrigill came from Kirkland, or the west side of Crossfell, it is still incredible that the people of this valley habitually carried back their dead for a period of a thousand years afterwards.

This becomes all the more incredible when we remember the very early and

* Vide Wallace, Alston Moor, pp. 18-21.
† Vide, p. 27.

intimate connection between Garrigill and Alston,* where there was a Churchyard.

Again, suppose the graveyard at Garrigill was made about 1650, and that prior to that the Garrigill dead were carried to Kirkland, we should expect to find evidence of this in the Kirkland Registers if they go so far back. It is satisfactory to know that Kirkland Burial Registers begin in 1620. Well, is there any evidence between 1620 and 1650, or later, that the Garrigill dead were habitually carried to Kirkland? When I state that during the thirty years concerned there are no Garrigill burials recorded at Kirkland the deductions of Mr. Wallace are very seriously discredited.

But even all this is said on the assumption that there was no Churchyard at Garrigill, which has not been proved in the least.

Evidence has been produced from wills that burials took place at Garrigill

---

a whole century before the time assigned
by Wallace as the date of the formation
of the Churchyard.   These names all
belong to one family :—

Nicholas Lee,* of Garrigill	...	1573
Michael Lee, of Garrigill	...	1578
Paul Lee, of Alston Parish	...	1586
George Lee, of Garrigill	...	1605
Arthur Lee, of Garrigill	...	1625
Arthur Lee, of Garrigill	...	1629
Nicholas Lee, of Crossgill	...	1631†

The traditions recorded by Wallace
still survive. The old people of Kirkland
are quite as certain as those of Garrigill
of a former relationship between the two
places. One tradition is that Kirkland
parish included Kirkland, Blencarne, Culgaith, Skirwith, and Garrigill! In those
days, so gossip says, Kirkland had five
Churchwardens, one from each Chapelry!
Nor is this all, for we are told that

---

* The memory of this family is preserved in " Lee
House."   The Lee family was connected with the
Archers and Waltons.

† Communicated by G. H. Rowbotham of Manchester.

every Easter each Warden had to provide a pewter flagon of wine.

Further, the mountain* road between Kirkland and Garrigill can still, with care, be followed, and the path between Kirkland and Alston is not difficult to find. Within the memory of some still living, garden produce, &c., has been carried from Kirkland to Alston market over the mountain *via* Green Castle.

All this goes to show that there was a very real connection between Garrigill on the east and Kirkland on the west of Cross Fell. But this relationship could not have been *ecclesiastical*, at least, for the past eight hundred years, for, throughout that period, Garrigill has

---

*Two men, in the winter time, were once travelling from Garrigill to Kirkland. One suddenly caught sight of a moving mass of ice and snow, and called to his companion. But the alarm came too late! The other was caught by the avalanch and killed. This incident is noted in the Kirkland Register. Is this the origin of the story of the corpse being left on the mountain for a fortnight? (Vide p. 103).

always shared the fate and fortunes of Alston.

The association was, no doubt, of a family and social character, and the interments at Kirkland from Garrigill could only have been occasional not customary.

That Kirkland, up to 1650, was the burial ground for Garrigill is a tradition void of all evidence and contrary to ascertained facts. The origin and date of the "Kirk-Garth" at Garrigill must be left at present as an unsolved problem.

In 1893 a Cemetery was opened in Garrigill, and the Churchyard was also enlarged.

The account of the consecration of the Churchyard extention, and the Church portion of the Cemetery, is worth preserving. It is taken from the Magazine for November, 1893.

"The great event of the month for us has been the visit of our Bishop to consecrate our two burial grounds on Sunday, October 29th. The day was bitterly cold and there were several heavy showers of hail, not however during the actual outdoor services fortunately. The service at the Cemetery was first held, the proceedings being commenced at 10 a.m. by a procession headed by the Burial Board, and consisting of the Bishop preceded by the Registrar (Mr. John Booth) and the Rev. P. T. Lee, who carried the Bishop's Pastoral Staff, and followed by the Vicar (Rev. Dr. Rutherford), Church-wardens (Messrs. H. Millican and T. Renwick), Sidesmen (Messrs. H. Walton and J. Blacklock), Clerk (Mr. Jos. Shield), and Choir. The procession having gone slowly round the part to be consecrated repeating the 49th Psalm, a halt was made in a sheltered portion of the Cemetery where the Bishop recited the beautiful consecration prayers and Mr. Booth read the legal declaration of con-secration. A similar service was then held in the Churchyard, the members of the Extension Committee taking the place of the Burial Board at the head of the procession. At the conclusion the procession entered the Church singing the hymn "A few more years shall roll," and the Rev. P. T. Lee having intoned the morning Service, and Dr. Rutherford having read the lessons, the Bishop preached on St. John XI. 25. At the evening Service his Lordship preached on behalf of the Hospital Sunday Fund, taking again, as he pointed out, words spoken by our Lord to a woman, St. John IV. 24 The collections at the morning Service for Church Expenses amounted to £2 2s., at the evening for the Hospital Fund to £1 12s. It is needless to add that the congregations filled the Church at each service."

Wallace says: "The prejudice against burying the dead on the north side of the Church seems to have existed in Garrigill, for the south side is full of graves, none having been made on the north side."*

---

* Wallace, Alston Moor, p. 85.

This statement also requires modification.

When I built the north Vestry in 1901 I obtained the Chancellor's Faculty to remove any bodies which might be found in excavating for foundations. Remains were found and were reverently re-interred. Their discovery necessitated putting in deep concrete foundations.

There lies in the Churchyard the base of a Cross, which is perhaps one of the oldest things about the Church. The outside measurements are 2 feet by 16 inches, and the socket 8 inches by 6 inches and 7 deep.

"It was an ancient custom of the Saxon Nation on the estates of some of their nobles and great men to erect, not a Church, but the sign of the Holy Cross, dedicated to God, beautifully and honourably adorned, and exalted on high, for the common use of daily prayer." Thus we read in the life of St. Willebald.[*]

---

[*] Acta SS. Ord. Benedict, Sec. iii., par. 2.

The remains of such a cross may be seen to-day in the Churchyard of Kirkland. It is possible, and probable too, that such a cross stood at Garrigill.

One very curious custom, in connection with the burials at Garrigill, has been described to me by some of the old people. After leaving the Church the corpse was carried three times round the building before being conveyed to the grave.

I

CHAPTER XV.

THE DAY SCHOOL—THE BUILD-
ING—THE SCHOOL MASTER—RE-
PAIRS—THE SCHOOL 'FARMED'—
COST OF REPAIRS—GIRLS' SCHOOL—
SCHOOLS UNITED—THE MANAGERS
—CHAIRMAN—THE OLD SCHOOL
BUILDING — ACT OF 1902 — TYNE-
HEAD SCHOOL.

Originally there were two buildings
near the Church, on the N.W. and S.W.
corners of the Churchyard respectively.

One was the Parish Stable,* and the
other the Parochial School. The school
building still remains. It has been very
incorrectly described as built *on the Village
Green* It is built, obviously, on glebe
land, *opposite* The Green.

---

* Vide, p. 74.

THE OLD SCHOOL-HOUSE, GARRIGILL.

Opp. p. 114.

The School house was rebuilt about a century ago.

"Garrigill Gate, June 2, 1809.

At a vestry meeting held at Garrigill Chapel this day it is unanimously agreed to take down, and enlarge the school-house, at Garrigill Gate, as witness our hands—

Churchwardens { Thomas Smith.
             { John Curragh.

Ralph Vipond.   George Swindle.
Isaac Vipond.   John Little.
John Vipond.   John Bradell.
John Watson.   Isaac Hall.
John Whitfield.   Francis Whitfield."

The builder was William Bell, who died during the progress of the work. On September 14, 1811, One Hundred and Forty One Pounds was paid by the Trustees "on account" to Thomas Bell, as Administrator for his brother William. I have failed to discover the total cost.

The earliest record of this school, I

think, is the Wilkinson Bequest of 1685,* but probably the school had been in existence for nearly one hundred and fifty years previously.

One of the early papers is a form of receipt for the Schoolmaster's stipend.

On " March ye 9th, 1757," we have the following :—

" Then received of Wm. Archer† the sume of five shillings in full of all accounts for Techeing Scoule att Garrigill.

I say received by me, STEPHEN COWPER."

The paper is endorsed, " Step. Cowper ; acquittance in full."

Some may hope that the good man "learned"‡ his scholars better than he spelt. But upon examination it looks as though the Church Warden had written

---

* Vide, Chapter xvii.   † The Church Warden.

‡ This use of the verb is not uncommon among the Cumbrian folk.

out the form of the receipt, and the Schoolmaster was responsible only for his own
signature, which is certainly pleasing, if
taken alone. Whatever be the term
covered by the five shillings, the payment
of this village pedagogue was very scanty.
But this, to a great extent, may be very
easily explained. Schoolmasters and even
parish priests in these remote parts were
received at the tables of the parishioners
at pre-arranged times, in order to help
them to eke out their nominal stipends.
In some parts this practice was in use
until the middle of the XIX century. The
name given to this custom in the dales
was *whittlegeat.*

A voluntary contribution was made
for the repair of the school in April, 1765.

There are 43 names on the list, and
the total sum amounts to £0 19s. 9d.

---

* Whittle—knife ; geat—sustenance (Vide p 5.) The
visitor brought his own knife.

One pound was expended on the building in 1777 :—

	£	s.	d.
For repairing Schoolhouse—			
For a door	0	4	0
Jos. Thompson, Glazing the Schoolhouse ...	0	1	0
Robt. Bell working lime ...	0	1	0
Isaac Winskell for lime ...	0	1	6
Edward Rain leading lime ...	0	1	0
James Robinson for hair ...	0	2	0
John Waugh for repairing the Schoolhouse	0	9	6
	£1	0	0

Sometimes the Schoolmaster was permitted to farm the school and pay rent to the Church Wardens, who were ex-officio Trustees of the building.

Three entries will suffice to illustrate this :

1777. "Robert Bell paid John Davidson rent for the Schoolhouse, due Martinmas last, £1 os. od."

1778. "Robert Bell paid Joseph Winskill rent for the schoolhouse, due Martinmas last, £1 0s. 0d."

1779. "Robert Bell paid Joseph Winskill rent for the Schoolhouse, due Martinmas last, £1 0s. 0d."

Passing to the next century the following items are of interest :—

"Garrigill Gate,
Feb 1st, 1804.

At a vestry meeting this day, held pursuant to public notice given, it is unanimously agreed that Thomas Vipond is to have the school, at this place, that belongs to the parish, to enter upon it this day, upon the same terms of the late master, Mr. Jno. Dickenson had, on condition that the said Thomas Vipond shall deliver up the key at the end of every three months either to Mr. Hodgson of Alston, or some other of the trustees whom he thinks proper to appoint.

(Signed)

*Robt. Hodgson.	Thomas Vipond.†
John Dickinson.	Samuel Hudspith.†
Utrick Walton.	Benj. Jackson, Vicar.
Thos. Vipond.	Francis Whitfield.
John Bell.	Isaac Vipond.
John Dickinson.	John Kindred.

I, Thomas Vipond, do agree to the above conditions.

Witness my hand,
Thomas Vipond."

1816—"Advertisements for a Schoolmaster, £1 10s. 0d."

"December 25th, 1820.

At a meeting held in the Chapple at Garrigill Gate this day, that it is fully determined that the school-house be kept in repair out of the Church 'cess."

---

* Secretary to the Trustees.   † Church Wardens.   .

"August 19th, 1825.

Church and School Repairs, £2 10s. od."

"September, 1828.

Paid to William Gill for repairing Church⁻ and School-house, per contract, £6 6s. od."

"Dr. to John Dryden for advertising in Carlisle 'Patriot' for School-master, 7s. od."

"Dr. to Jona. Robinson fo (?) advertising in Newcastle papers for School-master; 13s. od."

"Dr. to John Lowes for putting up School Tabel, repairing same, and wood for Church, per bill, £1 14s. 3d."

"Dr. to Ann Spark and Molly Modling for white-washing School, 5s. od."

"1848—Mr. J. Dryden for advertising for a School-master, £1 10s. od."

"1849—Dr. to Matthew Armstrong, repairing Church and School, 10s. 6d."

In 1848 a Library for the use of the mining population was built at Gate Foot—the extremity of the village towards Redwing.

Two years later a Girls' School was built on a contiguous plot, and a site containing two roods and embracing the two buildings—Girls' School and Library— was conveyed to Trustees by the Commissioners of the Greenwich Hospital.

The Trustees of this School were:—

William Paull, Lowbyre, Alston, Mining
　　　　Agent.
Tinniswood Millican, Nenthead, Mining
　　　　Agent.
Joseph Walton, Red Brow, Mining Agent.
George Millican, Tynehead, Mining Agent.
Joseph Pearson Slack, Lee House, Mining
　　　　Agent.
Jacob Smith, Bleagate, Miner.
Thomas Dobson, Garrigill Gate.
Joseph Renwick, the younger, of Eshgill
　　　　Side.
Matthew Hill of Craig.

Thomas Watson of Crooks.
George Dodd of Garrigill Gate.
Thomas Bowman of Redwing.
John Bramwell of Shield Hill.
William Bell of Dryburn.
Joseph Pickering of Garrigill Gate; and
John Bell of Tynehead, all also in the
Parish of Alston.

In 1874[*] the Girls' School and the old Parochial School united. The Trustees of the Girls' School wished to resign, and applied to the Board of Charity Commissioners on 19th August, 1873, to be discharged. This was accordingly done. The Trustees at that time were:

Joseph Renwick, Ashgill Side.
Matthew Hill, High Craig.
George Millican, Tynehead.
John Bramwell, Bishop Auckland.
William Bell, Dryburn.
Thomas Watson, Nenthead.
Tinniswood Millican, Nenthead.

---

* Wallace (Alston Moor), incorrectly says 1872, p. 80.

Joseph Walton, Alston.

Thomas Bowman, Alston.

The following members of the Trust, as constituted in 1850, were either dead, or could not be found:

William Paull.	John Bell.
Thomas Dobson.	Joseph Pearson Slack.
George Dodd.	Jacob Smith.
Joseph Pickering.	

The Acting Trustees of the Parochial School, *i.e.*, the Churchwardens and the Secretary, neither resigned, nor were they discharged.

The Churchwardens at this time were Isaac Curragh and John Slack. Joseph Watson was Secretary.

Under the scheme of the Charity Commissioners, the Managers of the United Schools at Gatefoot were:

1. The principal officiating minister of the Chapelry.

2. The Churchwardens of the Chapelry.

3.   Twelve other persons :

Rev. George Monkhouse, Clerk in
  Holy Orders.
Thomas Shaw, Shield Hill.
Joseph Watson, Crossgill.
George Pickering, Bridge End.
William Hutchinson. Lane Head.
William Bell, Dry Burn,
John Swindle, Middle Houses.
Jonathan Carr, Bunker's Hill,
Henry Walton, How Burn.
James Vipond, Garrigill.
Matthew Raisbeck, Red Brow.
Joseph Vipond, Garrigill.

About this time (1874) the Deeds of
the Parochial School *disappeared.* I found
a tradition current in the village concerning this document, but charity claims
that, in absence of positive evidence, the
rumour should die.

A slight change was made in 1898.
The Board of the Charity Commissioners
decided that the resident curate is the
principal officiating minister, and ex-

officio chairman within the meaning of
the scheme.

The vacated Parochial School building at the north-west corner of the
churchyard became, under this scheme, a
Library, Reading Room, and Mechanics'
Institute, instead of the building at Gate-
foot built in 1848.

The managing committee of the
organisation carried on here is elected by
the members.

The committee of the United Schools
at Gatefoot was affected by the Education Act of 1902. The number of members
was reduced to six. The resident clergyman and three elected persons formed the
Foundation Managers. The other two
seats were assigned to a representative of
the County Council and a representative
of the District Council.

There is another school in the
Chapelry—at Tynehead. There is evidence of this school being in existence for

a considerable period. For many years
the Rev. George Monkhouse (1851-1876)
was the Schoolmaster there, and very often
do middle aged residents refer with joy
and gratitude to the days when they were
his scholars.

CHAPTER XVI.

THE ARCHDEACON'S VISITATIONS
—1763—1768—1887.

Garrigill Chapel has been regularly visited by the Archdeacon like a parish church.

This is the record entered by the Archdeacon in 1763.*

"That the Table of Marriages be renewed; a new cover for the Font be procured; a new carpet for the Communion Table, and also a new cloth. That the hole for the bell be contracted; the flagging near the west door be made even; the roof strengthened and pointed; the broken seats repaired, and that those which are awry be set straight. That a

---

* Vide, p. 61.

book of Homilies be provided. That the cracked bell be new cast, or changed away and a bell of the same weight be provided. That all the pews and seats in the body of chapel and gallery be provided with moveable kneeling boards. That the arch under which the bell hangs be repaired, and the chapel yard provided with a new gate, which should be painted to preserve it. That the roof of the chancel be strengthened, new slated and painted."

There are several interesting matters in the entry made by the Archdeacon in 1768:

"On Wednesday, the 12th day of October, 1768, the Right Worshipful John Sharp, D.D., Archdeacon of the Archdeaconry of Northumberland, personally visited the Chapel of Garragill, in the Parish of Alstone, and directed and ordered as follows, to wit:

"That the ridge of the Roof at the West end of the Chapel be repaired.

K

"That the Arch where the Bell hangs be repaired and made more decent.

"That all the Pews in the Chapel, Chancel, and Gallery be furnished with moveable keeling boards, low or flat, and all the seats or benches furnished with fixed kneeling boards, low and flat.

"That a book of Homilies be provided, and a new Prayer-Book for the Clerk.

"That the Communion Table be decently repaired, and the minister's Bible new bound.

"That the Walls of the Chapel yard be put into proper repair, and the coping thereof pointed with lime.

"That the Styles into the Chapel yard be built up and the Gate repaired, and that a lock be put upon the Gate, and the same be kept locked at all proper times.

"That the Commandments be painted on wood, framed and hung up adjoining to each end of the Communion-Table.

"That the heaps of rubbish round the Chapel and Chancel be effectually removed, and that all the stones in the Chapel yard, not properly head stones or monuments, be removed out of the Chapel yard.

"That the Chapel be plastered where necessary, and the whole thereof, with the Chancel, whitewashed. That a Bason* for the Font, and a new Surplice be provided.

"And monished John Parmerley, one of the Chapel Wardens of the said Chapely, then and there present, and attending him in and during his said visitation, to do and perform, or cause to be done and performed, the several matters and things above mentioned, with all convenient speed, and to certify the performance thereof to him or some other competent judge at his next general visitation, to be holden after Easter next.

JOHN SHARP,
Archdeacon."

* See page 63.

Twenty years ago the Archdeacon recommended the entire separation of Garrigill from Alston.

"1887.

"Oct. 31.—Visited Garrigill Chapel with the Vicar and Curate of Alston. A Curate with special charge of Garrigill Chapel and District ought to reside in the Parsonage * here, and the chapel ought to be restored and a chancel added. The Churchyard ought to be enlarged by a portion of the lands on the East and South. When the things have been accomplished, the separation of Garrigill from Alston ought to be undertaken, for this ought certainly to form a separate parish.

GEO. HANS HAMILTON,
Archd. of Northumberland."

All the improvements advised by the Archdeacon have been carried out, but the issue—complete independence—has not been accomplished.

---

* At this time the clergyman from Nenthead acted as Curate.

CHAPTER XVII.

CHARITABLE BEQUESTS — JOHN
SHIELD, 1617—ROBERT WILKINSON,
1685—FAIRHILL ESTATE, 1739 AND
PREVIOUSLY — JOHN STEPHENSON,
1759 — AN UNKNOWN DONOR —
CHARLES ATWOOD, 1875.

There are several benefactions in which
the people of Garrigill are interested.

The following details are chiefly
abstracted from a Report of the Charity
Commissioners :—

I.—SHIELD'S GIFT.

John Shield, of London, by indenture,
dated 5th June, 1617, gave 40s. a year
to the poor of the Parish of Alston.

This sum is paid annually by the
Cooks' Company, London,* and is dis-

---

* A more particular account of this Donation is
given in the Report of the Charities vested in or under
the management of the Cooks' Company.

tributed amongst the poor of Alston and
Garrigill on Christmas Day, yearly; two-
thirds being given to the former, and one-
third to the latter place.

II.—WILKINSON'S CHARITY.

Robert Wilkinson, by Will, dated
24th February, 1685, gave £100 to the
village of Garrigill, where his mother
was born, to purchase lands of the clear
yearly value of £5 to be disposed of in
the following manner, viz. :—20s. a year
to a Schoolmaster at Garrigill towards his
maintenance, and 40s. a year to the said
Schoolmaster for teaching six poor children
of the poorest inhabitants of Garrigill—
gratis—till they could read the Bible
through, and then others to be put in
their stead; 10s. to a Minister for preaching a sermon every year in Garrigill
Chapel on the first day of February; and
10s. to be distributed yearly to such poor
inhabitants in Garrigill, as his trustees
and their successors should judge most
needful, in the said Chapel, immediately
after the said sermon; and the remaining

20s. a year to his four trustees, and their successors, to each of them 5s. a piece. Provided always, that if the said trustees and their successors should neglect or refuse to nominate and appoint six poor children, to be taught as aforesaid, for the space of one month after they should be desired by the said Schoolmaster, then the said 40s. a year, left for their learning, and the said 20s. a year, left to the said trustees, should, for ever after, be paid to the said Chapelwardens and Overseers of the Poor, and should be by them distributed yearly and every year to the poor in the said Chapel, upon the 1st day of February, in manner aforesaid.

In 1689, this sum was laid out in the purchase of an annuity or rent-charge of £5, issuing out of certain premises situate in Bowes, in the county of York, for the uses of the said will, which is now paid regularly by the Rev. John Headlam, Rector of Wycliffe, the owner of the property. Twenty shillings are paid to the Schoolmaster at Garrigill, and 40s.

more for teaching six poor children there, gratis, who are appointed by the trustees. The Vicar of Alston receives 10s. yearly for preaching a Sermon in the chapel of Garrigill; and on that same day, 10s. are distributed to the poor people there. The remaining 20s. are retained by the trustees for their own use.

III.—FAIRHILL ESTATE, INCLUDING MRS. GRAHAM'S GIFT.

By indenture dated 15th September, 1739, between John Friend, of Annot Walls, of the first part; Thomas Vipont and others, Churchwardens and Overseers of the parish, of the second part; and Nicholas Whitfield and others of the third part.

Reciting, that there had theretofore been bequeathed to the poor of the parish of Alston, to the School in Alston, and to the poor and School within the chapelry of Garrigill, several sums of money, amounting in the whole to £217 5s. od. of which there belonged:—

To the poor of Alston........£83 6 8
To the School in Alston.... 81 5 0
To the poor of Garrigill. .. 27 13 4
To the School in Garrigill. 25 0 0

£217 5 0

And reciting, that the Churchwardens, Overseers, and inhabitants of the said parish, for the better securing the said charities, had contracted for the purchase of the premises thereinafter mentioned, and that they had ordered the same to be conveyed to John Friend in trust, to be by him assigned to such persons as should be by them afterwards appointed; and reciting, that Nicholas Whitfield and others of the third part, had been appointed by them trustees. It is witnessed, that the said John Friend, in consideration of five shillings, conveyed to the said trustees a messuage or tenement, with the appurtenances, at Nether Fair Hill, in Alston Moor, being freehold property, and assigned to them a fourth part of the pasture called Fairhill Pasture, in Alston

Moor, and an inclosure at Nether Fair Hill, adjoining the messuage above-mentioned, being leasehold property, held for the remainder of a term of 1,000 years, upon trust that they should let the same and apply the rents thereof in the following proportions :—

For the Overseer of poor of Alston,
    for the use of the poor of the
    said parish...........................£4 3 4
For the Schoolmaster of Alston.. 4 1 3
To the Overseers of Garrigill, for
    the use of the poor............... 1 7 8
To the Schoolmaster of Garrigill 1 5 0

And if the rents should amount to more or less, that an increase or deduction should be made from each part in the like proportions.

It appears that the whole of the consideration money was £274, of which £68 was to be paid for the completion of the purchase, within six months after the death of Mary Wallis, as may be collected from a bond, dated 8th May,

1738; and by indorsement thereon, the sum of £68 is stated to have been paid 4th September, 1756.

By identures of lease and release, dated 30th April and May 1st, 1756, the Trustees, Churchwardens, and Overseers mortgaged the premises to Ann Whitfield, for securing the sum of £68, which was probably raised for the completing the purchase as above-mentioned.

By indentures of lease or release, dated 19th and 20th June, 1797, reciting, the trustees were entitled to the several premises above-mentioned upon certain trusts, by means whereof they had become chargeable with the payment of £68 to Joseph Wallis, who called upon the trustees for the same; and reciting, that the said trustees had borrowed £68 of Ann Graham, formerly Ann Whitfield, and had mortgaged the premises above-mentioned as a security for the same and further reciting, that the said Ann Graham, by will, dated 4th April, 1796, had directed her executor, George Mowbray, within

12 months after her death, to assure the
£68 so secured as above-mentioned, in
such manner that the yearly interest
might be applied towards the augmentation of the salary of the master of the
School at Alston.

It is witnessed, that the said George
Mowbray conveyed and assigned the said
freehold and leasehold premises to Joseph
Thompson and other persons for the
remainder of a term that had been
vested in the said Ann Graham, upon
trust to apply the interest of the said
mortgage in augmentation of the salary
of the said Schoolmaster.

On the inclosure of Alston by Act of
Parliament, of 43rd, George III., allotments were made to this property in
respect of the freehold and lease-interests;
the former consisting of 43a. 1r. 32p. and
the latter in two parcel (one 3a. 1r. 6p.
the other 39a. 3r. 16p.) amounting in the
whole to 86a. 2r. 14p.

The above allotments (except about
two or three acres) are let on lease for

21 years, from 1st May, 1811, to William
Pearson, at £16 a year. The letting was
by tender, public notice having been
previously given. The tenant is to make
boundry and sub-division fences, and to
lay not less than 2,200 Carlisle bushels
of Lime on the land within the last
seven years of his term, and to keep all
fences and gates in repair.

The original Fairhill Estate, consisting
of 22 acres, together with about two or
three acres of the new allotment, is let
to Mary Yates for one year, at £36 10s. 0d.
This estate has lately been let yearly to
the best bidder, and is generally let to
the person who has the care of the poor,
the workhouse being situated on this
estate.

We have particulary inquired, whether
this estate is not let for a less value, by
reason that the person who takes the land
also agrees to farm the poor at a certain
rate. It appears, however, that this land
is let at its full value, and that the
allowance for the poor varies with the

times. We find, that in 1818 the estate was let at £30 a year, the tenant farming the poor at 2s. 10d. per head per week. In 1819, £35 was the rent of the land, and the poor were taken at 2s. 8d. In the present year, as before stated, £36 10s. is the rent, and the poor are taken at 2s. 5d. by which it appears that the rent has increased regularly, whilst the allowance for the poor has diminished.

The poor-house is supposed to have been built long ago at the expense of the parish, by whom it is now repaired. No rent is allowed by the parish in respect of the occupation of these premises which seem to supply the place of a farm-house for the land.

The application of these rents is very irregular, the whole having been carried to the general account of the parish poor-rate for several years. On the other hand, there have been payments made thereout to the Schoolmasters of Alston and Garrigill. For the last few years these payments have been—

To the Schoolmaster of Alston £26 4 0
To the Schoolmaster of Garrigill 7 0 10½

Whilst the remainder has been improperly applied to the general purposes of the parish.

We could not discover by what calculation the Schoolmaster received these several sums, which are not in proportion to the scale drawn out in the indenture of 1739. It does not appear whether interest for the sum of £68 given by Mrs. Graham, is included in the payment to the Schoolmaster at Alston, but it probably forms a part of his salary.

For the last year nothing has been paid to either of the Schoolmasters. A demand of about £70 has been made by the Commissioners for the expenses incurred relating to the inclosure. A former demand of £69 9s. 6d., for the same purpose, was paid out of the Poor Rate— but several of the parishioners have objected to the payment of this second demand, and, until this question is settled, the payment to the Schoolmasters has been withheld. But, considering that for several years the parish has received the benefit of the surplus, which ought to have been distributed in charity to the poor, we trust there will be no difficulty in this respect, and that, in future, a more correct distribution will be made of the rents of this property, according to the scale laid down in the Trust Deed; first setting apart £3 8s. as the specific interest of Mrs. Graham's legacy, to be paid to the Schoolmaster of Alston.

The Alston Schoolmaster receives all children coming to him at quarterage settled by the Vestry, which is considered a lower rate than would be paid if the School had no endowment. Six children were formerly taught free; but for the last four or five years the Parish has not insisted upon the Master teaching any children gratuitously.

No children are taught free for the share paid to the Schoolmaster at Garrigill.

Since this report was drawn up, we have been informed by the Vicar of Alston, that it has been agreed at a Vestry Meeting, that the rent of the Fairhill Estate, as far as relates to the poor of the Parish of Alston, shall, in future, be applied, and given by the Churchwardens and Overseers, to such poor persons as have not received parochial relief; and that two persons are to be appointed to survey the estate and ascertain the rent, in order that each establishment may receive its due proportion.*

---

* This and all similar benefactions are affected by the Education Act of 1902. 2 Edw. 7, Ch. 42, 13 (1).

" Nothing in this Act shall affect any endowment, or the discretion of any trustees in respect thereof: Provided that, where under the trusts or other provisions affecting any endowment the income thereof must be applied in whole or in part for those purposes of a public elementary school for which provision is to be made by the local education authority, the whole of the income or the part thereof, as the case may be, shall be paid to that authority, and, in case part only of such income must be so applied and there is no provision under the said trusts or provisions for determining the amount which represents that part, that amount shall be determined, in case of difference

L

IV.—STEPHENSON'S CHARITY.

John Stephenson, by Will, dated 29th
May, 1759, desired his executor, Matthew
Stephenson, out of his personal estate to
which he would be entitled by the said
Will, to pay yearly and every year for
ever, to and amongst 16 poor widows
who should have legal settlements in the
Parish of Aldstone and Chapelry of Garri-

---

between the parties concerned, by the Board of Education, but if a public inquiry is demanded by the local
education authority, the decision of the Board of
Education shall not be given until after such an
inquiry, of which ten day's previous notice shall be
given to the local education authority and to the
minor local authority and to the trustees, shall have
been first held by the Board of Education at the cost
of the local education authority

"Any money arising from an endowment and
paid to a county council for those purposes of a
public elementary school for which provision is to be
made by the council, shall be credited by the council
in aid of the rate levied for the purposes of this Part
of this Act in the parish or parishes which in the
opinion of the council are served by the school for
the purposes of which the sum is paid, or, if the
council so direct, shall be paid to the overseers of
the parish or parishes in the proportions directed by
the council, and applied by the overseers in aid of
the poor rate levied in the parish"

gill, in the county of Cumberland, 5s. each ; and to 8 poor widows who should have legal settlements in the parish of Knarsdale; and also to 8 poor widows who should have legal settlements in the parish of Kirkhaugh, both in the county of Northumberland, 5s. each ; and for want of such a number of poor widows in the said chapelry and parishes respectively, his will and desire was, that such number might be from time to time made up and supplied, and the said respective annual sums paid to and amongst so many poor men respectively, having legal settlements in the said chapelry and parishes respectively, as the number of poor widows should respectively fall short, the same to them and every one of them at Aldstone, Knarsdale, and Kirkhaugh respectively, on the 25th day of December in every year, by the minister and churchwardens, for the time being, of those places respectively. And he did also desire the said Matthew Stephenson, his executors and administrators, to distribute yearly and every year, on the

25th day of December for ever, to eight
poor persons having legal settlements in
the Parish of Boldon, in the county of
Durham, 5s. a piece, and he willed that
during the life of his wife the proper and
deserving objects of that charity might
be determined by her and the said
Matthew Stephenson And to the end
that the said charities before-mentioned
might be continued for ever, he, the said
John Stephenson, did desire the said
Matthew Stephenson would, immediately
after his death, charge the house in
Westgate Street, in Newcastle aforesaid,
tenanted by Mrs Lyddell, with the annual
sum of £10 for ever, according to the
directions of the Act of Parliament in
that case made and provided, so that a
perpetual fund might subsist for the
aforesaid charities

By indenture, dated 18th July, 1761,
enrolled in the Court of Chancery, the
said Matthew Stephenson being desirous
to fulfil the charitable intent of the said
testator, granted to Ogle Wallis and
William Peters, their heirs and assigns,

a rent-charge of £10 issuing out of all that brick messuage, burgage or tenement in Westgate Street, Newcastle, purchased by the said John Stephenson of George Graham deceased, in trust, for the purposes mentioned in the said will.

The sum of £4 is regularly received from John Annerdale, Esq., who is the possessor of the house in Westgate Street, Newcastle, £2 are given to 8 poor widows having settlements in Alston, and the same sum to 8 in Garrigill Chapelry, under the direction of the Vicar of Alston, who has regularly attended to the distribution for the last 30 years.*

V —DONOR UNKNOWN

In the returns to Parliament in 1786, a sum of money belonging to this Chapelry, producing 10s. yearly as interest, is stated to be " lent on a promissory note, and the security bad." No donor's name or date is given.

---

* The date of the Charity Commission Report is 1834.

On inquiry we find that there was a sum of money lent on note, but that the person who had it died insolvent many years ago, and nothing could be recovered.

There is no doubt that the following paper, preserved in the Church Safe, refers to these moneys:—

"We do jointly and severally promise to pay to Robert Bland and William Archer, Churchwardens, for the parish of Garrigill, or to their succeeding Officers the sum of Fourteen pounds upon demand with lawful interest for the same for valley *(sic)* received, as witness our hands this 29th day of January, 1757.

Joseph Clocker,
John Clocker,
Witness: Isaac Vipond." [*]

VI.—ATWOOD'S CHARITY.

VI.—By his will, dated 12th February, 1875, Charles Atwood, of Wolsingham,

---

[*] Churchwarden the following year.

left £25 per annum to be paid to the
Vicar of Alston for the benefit of the
poor, at the discretion of the Vicar for
the time being, but without reference
to any religious distinction.   A sum of
money, producing £25, was to be invested
in land, stock, or the public funds, and
the interest was to be paid yearly to
the Vicar by the Trustees of the invested
capital.   Garrigill participates in this
benefaction to the extent of about £5
yearly ·

---

* Catherine Emerson of Eshgill made a curious will
dated May 20, 1712. She gave two pounds to the poor
of Garrigill, the interest to be distributed at " Martinmas,"
each year. This also appears to have been lost. Vide
Appendix C.

CHAPTER XVIII.

FAMILY HISTORY AND BIOGRAPHY —THE VIPONDS—THE ARCHERS— THE WALTONS—PROSPEROUS DAYS —LONG LIVES — JOHN TAYLOR — WESTGARTH FORSTER — BLYTHE HURST—JOSEPH SHIELD—A GENERAL LIST.

The Registers testify that the principal family names of the Chapelry are Vipond, Archer, and Walton, names which to-day are well-nigh extinct.

I. Vipond * The Viponds claim that they are not the descendants of the retainers, but the lineal offspring of the Norman house of Veteri Ponte. This ancient name has almost disappeared. Some 200 years ago there were families of this name in every part of the Chapelry. They were to be found in the village, and

---

* I have discussed the origin of this name in Chapter II.

VIPOND ARMS.

Or., Six Annulets Gules.

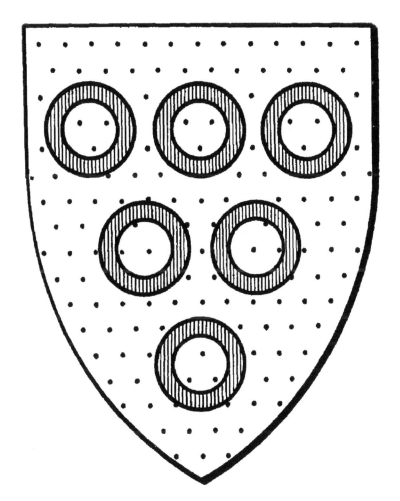

Plate presented by Miss Vipond, London.

in homesteads on both sides of the Tyne. Driburn, Skydes, Rotherhope, Gatefoot, Gatehead, Crossgill, Lee House, Flatt, Craigshield, Fewsteads, Upper Craig, Middle Craig, Low Craig, and Loaning Head were all homes of the Viponds at the beginning of the XVIII. Century.

1. Driburn was occupied by Thomas Vipond. His father, also Thomas, and his mother, Elizabeth, both died there in 1706. Thomas, the younger, remained in the house, at least, till 1729. One child (Mary) was born in August, 1722, and died in the summer of the following year. The other children were Thomas (1709), John (1714), Joseph (1716), Nicholas (1719), Elizabeth (1724), and Jane (1729). There is a legend concerning this house of an old gentleman who wore silver buckles bearing the Vipond arms on his shoes.*

2. Rotherhope was held by Nicholas Vipond who died in 1720. His wife, Sarah, died in child-bed nearly nine

---

* Vide opposite illustration.

years previously. The child only out-lived the mother about ten days, and had received the name Rachael. The other children appear to have died also. Their names were Isaac, William, Mary, Nathan, and Thomas.

3. Skydes was also held by a Vipond named Thomas. Thomas was a favourite name among the Viponds. A child of this home was baptized as Thomas in July, 1716, but in the following February this infant died. The name was revived, being given to a child baptized in November, 1720. Two little girls of this home Grace, aged 8, and Hannah, aged 3, were buried in the same grave, on September 14, 1726. The other children were Anne (1713), Joshua (1726), and Mary (1728).

4. There was also a family at Gate-foot. Arthur Vipond was resident here from 1713 to 1716. His daughter Hannah was baptised in the former year, and his son Joseph in the latter. I think I can also trace him as living at Low Craig,

Redwing, and Driburn. If so, he must have been a younger son of the family.

Thomas Vipond died here April 19, 1761, and his will was proved 1762.

John Vipond, son of Thomas, died Feb. 17, 1787, and his will was proved August 31, 1787. The other children of Thomas were Mary, Thomas, Joseph, Isaac, and Hannah.

Thomas Vipond, son of John, was born November 17, 1758. He was married July 8, 1782, and buried August 25, 1824.* The other children of John were Mary, Hannah, Rachel, and Margaret.

William Vipond, son of Thomas, was born October, 9, 1796. He married twice, first Isabella Dickinson, and then Jane Elliott. The children of Jane Elliott were Susannah Jane, John, Thomas, and Sarah. He died at Middleton-in-Teasdale February 28, 1857. The other children of Thomas were Thomas, Mary, Isaac, Sarah, John and Joseph.

---

* He was Schoolmaster. Vide, pp. 119-120,

William Dickinson Vipond, son of William Vipond, by Isabella Dickinson was born at Middleton-in-Teasdale, May 29, 1835, and died in 1882.[*]

5. Gatehead was the home of Jacob Vipond. He took to wife one of his own clan—Mary Vipond—in 1715.

We know of two sons of this marriage Thomas born in 1719, and Nicholas in 1723.

Mary died in 1726, and her husband in 1727.

There were two or three other Vipond familes living here. One of these was the household of Nicholas Vipond. There seems to be no record of surviving children Another family was that of Thomas Vipond and his wife Lydia. They both died in the same year—1718. This family, too, seems to have expired. Ann was buried in 1717. Thomas and Mary (a girl of 15 years) both died in 1726.

---

[*] I have received some of these details from Miss Vipond, of Plumstead.

Let us glance at some of the homesteads on the other side of the river

6.   At Middle Craig lived John Vipond
and his wife Hannah, who had thrown in
their lot with the Nonconformists Hannah
had three children, John (1720), Elizabeth
(1722), and Hannah (1724).   Five months
after the birth of the last named child
the mother died.   Within twelve months
John married again, his second wife being
Margaret Harrison, of Low Houses, and
she appears to have shaken John's
Nonconformist ideas.   They had two
children Elizabeth (1726) and Joseph
(1727), one of which was baptised at
Church.

7.   Low Craig was occupied by Arthur
Vipond in 1708.   He also lived at different times at Driburn, Redwing, and Gate-
foot.   His children were John (1711),
Hannah (1713), Joseph (1716), Elizabeth
(1717), and Grace (1720.) William died
in infancy—born 1708, died 1710.

8.   At Loaning Head lived Nicholas
Vipond. His wife, Abigail, died in 1708,

and he out-lived her exactly a year. Their children were Joseph (1705) and Thomas (1708). The latter appears to have become a father at 18, and his child received the name of his mother, Abigail.

John Vipond also lived here. His children were Nicholas (1720), William (1723), and Mary (1726).

The women of the Viponds at this time married into these families among others—White, Marshall, Hodgson, Teasdale, Stagg, Baxter, Wallace, Brown, Bell, and Archer. There were other branches of the Viponds besides those referred to in these notes.

II. Archer. The first name in the Garrigill Burial Register (1699) is that of Archer. The origin of this family has been carefully sketched by Mr. G. H. Rowbotham.

1. In the year 1228 for services duly rendered John le Archer received a grant of 40 acres of land in Allendale from

Walter de Grey, Archbishop of York, and it is possible this John was the original progenitor of the stock in South Tynedale.

2.—In default of positive evidence it is necessary to come down another couple of centuries to another "John Archer of the parish of Aldneston," born there in the year 1453. He was living in 1522, when, described as yeoman, and aged 69, he appeared as a witness in a very curious suit of the Whitfield's at Durham. He is also mentioned in the Drift Roll of Alston Moor, made in the days of King Henry VII., and probably resident at Browneside, where, in the year 1610, his descendant Anthony Archer died and made his will.

3. At the Dissolution, the advowson of the Church of Alston accrued to the Crown, and sometime between the years 1547 and 1553 King Edward VI. gave to Arthur Lee, of Craig Hall, and Thomas Archer "the rectory, glebe, advowson, and gift of the vicarage of Alston to

pertain to them and their heirs for ever" These gentlemen associated with them Sir Thomas Hilton, Knight, and the three presented in turn. This Thomas Archer "of Blaegate in Alestone Moor" died in the year 1584, and was buried in the private chapel of the Barons Hilton at Hilton.

4. "William Archer of Alston Moor Esquire," son of the preceding, presented to the Church of Alston in 1624 and again in 1625.

5. Nearly quarter of a century later (in 1649) John Archer of Whitthill (Whittle), Shilbottle parish, Northumberland, bequeathed to his wife, for the maintenance of his young children, all his Tithe in the parish of Austin Moore.

6. In the year 1665 Jane Archer, one of the two children above mentioned, married Moses Henzell, of "Newcastle Glasshouse." This gentleman, by inheritance or purchase, then became possessed of the advowson and appears as patron of the living in 1696.

7. Anthony Archer, a younger brother of Thomas Archer of " Blagate," resided in the Chapelry of Garrigill, and died there in 1586. His descendants were living at the farms of Tynehead and "Sheall" Hill in the latter half of the 18th century.

8. Soon afterwards, the hard times then prevailing drove most of the members of this branch of the family from their ancient seed plot, and its present representatives are now to be found in Rothbury, London, Manchester, and far distant America.*

The following table gives the descent of Ralph Archer, the first to be entered in the Burial Register of Garrigill :—

---

* Other appearances of the name in the North —
1. Archbishop Giffard of York (1226-1279) was related to ARCHER (Aucher).
2 There were Archers of Eastington, Durham.
3. Also at Oxenholme, Westmorland. Vide Burke and Nicholson.
4. There is an Archer Monument in Wetheral Church (1789).

M

ARCHER.

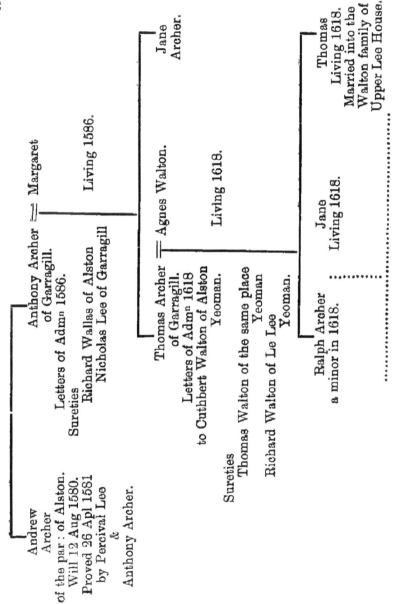

Andrew Archer of the par: of Alston. Will 12 Aug 1580. Proved 26 Apl 1581 by Percival Lee & Anthony Archer.

Anthony Archer of Garragill. = Margaret Living 1586.
Letters of Admn 1586. Sureties Richard Wallas of Alston Nicholas Lee of Garragill

Jane Archer.

Thomas Archer of Garragill. = Agnes Walton. Living 1618.
Letters of Admn 1618 to Cuthbert Walton of Alston Yeoman.
Sureties Thomas Walton of the same place Yeoman Richard Walton of Le Lee Yeoman.

Thomas Living 1618. Married into the Walton family of Upper Lee House.

Jane Living 1618.

Ralph Archer a minor in 1618.

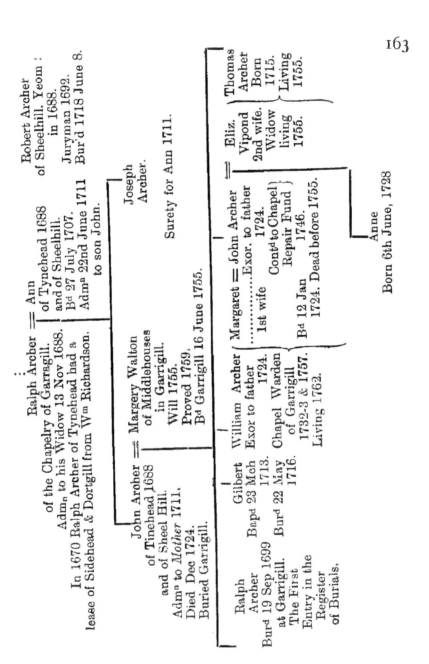

Ralph Archer = Ann
of the Chapelry of Garragill.   of Tynehead
Adm^n to his Widow 13 Nov 1688.   and of Sheelhill.
In 1670 Ralph Archer of Tynehead had a   B^d 27 July 1707.
lease of Sidehead & Dortgill from Wm Richardson.   Adm^n 22nd June 1711
to son John.

Robert Archer
of Sheelhill. Yeom :
in 1688.
Juryman 1692.
Bur'd 1718 June 8.

Joseph
Archer.

Surety for Ann 1711.

John Archer = Margery Walton
of Tinehead 1688   of Middlehouses
and of Sheel Hill.   in Garrigill.
Adm^n to Mother 1711.   Will 1755.
Died Dec 1724.   Proved 1759.
Buried Garrigill.   B^d Garrigill 16 June 1755.

Margaret = John Archer   = Eliz.
1st wife   Exor. to father   Vipond
B^d 12 Jan   1724.   2nd wife.
1724. Dead before 1755.   Cont^d to Chapel   Widow
Repair Fund   living
1746.   1755.

William Archer
Exor to father
1724.
Chapel Warden
of Garrigill
1732-3 & 1757.
Living 1762.

Ralph
Archer
Bur^d 19 Sep 1699
at Garrigill.
The First
Entry in the
Register
of Burials.

Gilbert
Archer
Bapd 23 Mch
1713.
Bur^d 22 May
1716.

Thomas
Archer
Born
1715.
Living
1755.

Anne
Born 6th June, 1728

III. Walton. We are chiefly interested in this name through the public character of Reginald Walton of the commonwealth days, whose Latin epitaph lies inside the Church door.[*]

I shall confine my attention to his branch of the family.

These notes are complied chiefly from wills and deeds in the possession of J. R. Walton, J.P., of Alston; G. H. Rowbotham, of Manchester; J. Slack, B.A., of Birmingham, and others.

1. Nicholas Lee, of Garrigill, who had married Elizabeth Archer, a widow, gave, by will dated 1573, his lease of Lee House, to his step-daughter Elizabeth Archer. She was a minor in 1573, and probably became the wife of Richard Walton.

2. September, 1611, Henry Hilton, Esq. granted Richard Walton, of Upper Lee House, " the lease now enjoyed by John Vipond."

---

* Vide p. 97, and Chapter xix.

3. May 6th, 1612. The probate of the will of Richard Walton.

4. In 1618 Richard Walton, of Le Lee, Yeoman, and Thomas Walton, of the parish of Garrigill, were sureties to a bond to Cuthbert Walton, of Alston, Yeoman, for the benefit of the widow of Thomas Archer, of Garrigill, and her children.

5. In 1620 Reginald Walton, of Upper Lee House was born.

6. In 1629 Richard Walton was one of the Jurors appointed to copy the "Paine Roll."*

7. 1663 there is a deed which bears the signature of Reginald Walton. It is an indenture dated the 14th of May, 1663 between Nicholas Richardson and Joseph Richardson, his only son, by which the father transfers to his son certain lands, and money lent on mortgage, in the

* Vide Appendix D

Chapelry of Garrigill. This indenture is witnessed by John* Walton, Reginald Walton, and Robert Walton.

8. In 1665, Sept. 21, we have a deed of Richard Walton to Reginald Walton.†

9 In 1672 Reginald Walton is occupier of Upper Lee House, and his house was licensed for Puritan preaching.‡

10. Oct. 15th, 1691, deed of Reginald Walton in favour of John Walton and John Vipond.¶

---

* There is a deed dated 10th March, 1662 between John Walton, of Garrigill Gate, and his son Thomas Walton, and another between the said Thomas Walton and his mother Jane, made in the year 1680.

†It seems to me that there were two named Richard—1612 and 1665, and that the second Richard was father of Reginald. A claim, which has been urged, that Reginald was son of John Walton (Vide deed of 1663) is a conjecture based merely on John's name being first

‡ Vide p 97 and Chapter xix

¶ May 21st, 1691, a deed of John Walton to John Vipond.

11. 1706 Mary, the wife of Reginald Walton, buried Oct. 28.

12. 1713 Reginald Walton buried Aug. 4th.*

I do not attempt to construct any table from these items. I prefer to leave them in this form for the use of some other worker possessing additional facts.

THE SIGNATURE OF REGINALD WALTON †

---

* June 11, 1703 Ephraim Walton was buried.

May 11th, 1704 Reginald Walton, of Silly Hole was buried.

This Reginald is thought to be the son of Reginald, of Lee House, and the father of Ephraim who died the previous year.

† By permission of J. R. Walton, J.P.

The close of the eighteenth century and the opening years of the nineteenth century witnessed a period of great prosperity. The population then was more than three times the present number.* A Fair in Garrigill for black cattle, horses and sheep, was the annual resort of the country side. A reproduction of the bill, announcing The Fair, is given on the opposite page. There was also a Shot Factory in brisk operation.†

We should like to direct the attention of those interested in Garrigill to the number of people who have lived to a great age in this valley since 1800.

Alry Brown, who lived to 103, died in 1833.

Free entertainment was given to 1,100 people in Garrigill at a festival to celebrate the passing of the Reform Bill in 1832. The tables extended from High

---

* Vide Appendix E.

† Mrs James Vipond owns an agreement by which Thomas Shaw her father purchased a quarter share from Hugh Lee Pattison, June 8th, 1820.

Garrigill-Gate, July 26th, 1799.

To the Public.

A Fair will be held for Black-cattle, Sheep, and Horſes, on the firſt Friday in September, and alſo, on the third Friday in May, at Garrigill-Gate, in Alſtonmoor, and County of Cumberland.

N. B. The ſaid Fairs to be held annually.

ALSTON: PRINTED BY J. HARROP.

Butt Hill to Low Butt Hill on the Village Green. John Martin and his wife who were both 102 were put at the head of the table, Mary Martin being arrayed in her wedding dress.

The death of these old worthies is thus recorded in the Register :—

"John Martin Ashgill-Side died April 21st. 1834 aged 103."

"Mary Martin Ashgill-Side died Nov. 16th, 1836 aged 105."

The following are recorded in the Church Register, as being over 90:—Mary Tolson, Jane Dodd, Francis Robson, Sarah Archer, Mary Hodgson, Margaret Raine, Thomas Pearson, Elizabeth Watson, Mary Millican, Hannah Shield, Ann Smith, Mary Slack, Thomas Robinson, Ann Wallace, Elizabeth Hodgson, Simeon Moor, and Mary Phillipson.

The age of ninety in so many instances, speaks highly for the health of Garrigill, especially when we re-

THE VILLAGE GREEN.

The two figures show the site of the ancient Butts where the natives practiced archery.

member that the occupation of the men, lead mining, is by no means conducive to long life, and that the number of inhabitants has at no time been more than 1,700, and for many years has been below 1000.

I have a large collection of local biographies, far too large to be reproduced here. A selection must suffice, each case being in its way unique.

1. JOHN TAYLOR. In 1767 a paper was read before the Society of Antiquaries in London, concerning a native of Garrigill, who was at that time "alive and well," John Taylor, by name. His age was 130, and he lived for five years afterwards.

The paper states:—

"John son of Barnabas or Bernand (he calls him Barny) Taylor, by his wife Agnes Watson was born in Garrigill, in the parish of Aldston in Cumberland. His father was a miner, and he died

when John was four years old. At the
age of nine years, he was set to work
at dressing lead ore, which he followed
two years at twopence a day. He then
went below ground to assist the miners,
and had been thus employed for three
or four years, when the great solar
eclipse, vulgarly called "Mirk Monday"
happened Nov. 29th, 1652. He, being then
at the bottom of the shaft or pit, was
desired by the man at the top to call
those below to come out, because a
black cloud had darkened the sun so
that the birds were falling to the earth.
And this, which he always relates with
the same circumstances, is the only event
by which his age may be ascertained.
About the age of 15 he went to work at the
lead mines at Blackwall in the Bishop-
rick of Durham. He was afterwards
employed as a miner or overseer in the
island of Islay, where he continued till
1730, when he went to Glasgow. From
thence he came, in 1733, to Lead Hills,
where he wrought constantly, in the
mines till 1752 ; and has still the profit

of a bargain (about £8 or £10 per annum) from the Scots Mine Company, which supports him comfortably.

"His wife bore him nine children in Islay; four of whom died young. His eldest daughter was born in 1710, was married, and died in 1753. Two sons and two daughters are alive in this place (Lead Hills) and are married, except the youngest son born in 1730. His wife died in 1758.

"He was always a thin spare man, about five feet four inches, black haired, ruddy faced, and long visaged. As miners are obliged to work at all hours, he never found any difference of times, with regard to working, sleeping, or eating. His appetite is still good, but must have a glass of spirit, once or twice a day, to warm his stomach, as he expresses it. His sight and hearing are not greatly impaired. His hair is not more gray than that of people, generally, about fifty; but his eyebrows, remarkably bushy, and his beard, are entirely white. In

cold weather he lies much in bed; but
in the warm months he walks about
with a stick; and is very bowed down.
In October last he walked from his own
house to Lead Hill (a computed mile)
and having entertained his children and
grand children in a public house, he
returned the same day."

A further account relates :—

"The first sickness he remembers to
have had (for the small-pox he had in
his infancy) was about the year 1724
when he was seized with dysentry. He
had a fever in the Highlands which was
attended by one remarkable circumstance.
Having been let blood, the wound broke
open, and was not observed till the blood
had run through the bed and floor into
a lower room. The scurvy which seized
him there continued to afflict him for
several years after he came to Lead
Hills, and during his wife's illness, in
February 1758, he catched cold, which
brought him very low. But since his
recovery, he has not had the least com-

plaint, nor does he remember to have any sickness but what is above mentioned. He never slept much, and he says that when he was in Durham his business for four years was to attend a fire engine, during which time he was allowed no more than four hours sleep in the twenty-four, and he bore it well."

Taylor died in 1772 at the age of 135.

2. WESTGARTH FORSTER.

Westgarth Forster was a celebrated mineralogist and mining expert. His name is still a household word in Garrigill, and the surrounding district, as well as in other mining centres.

His work entitled "*A Treatise on the strata from Newcastle-upon-Tyne to Cross Fell with remarks on Mineral Veins, etc*"* is still regarded as a work of reference.

---

* A third revised edition was published by the Rev. W. Nall, M.A. in 1883.

N

Thomas Brown married Elizabeth Dickinson (widow, of Eshgill) *alias* Craig (Betty Brown). Up to April 23rd, 1790, their descendants numbered 436 persons.*

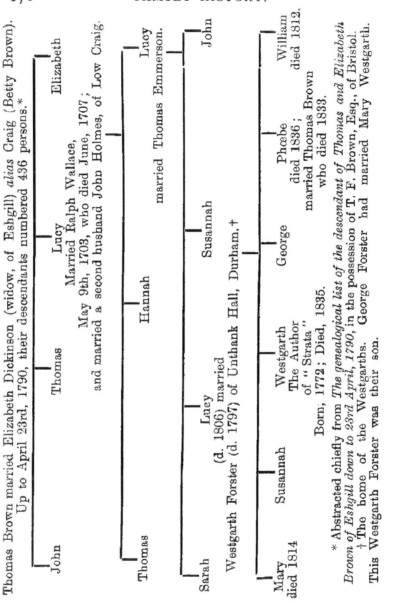

John

Thomas

Lucy
Married Ralph Wallace, May 9th, 1703, who died June, 1707; and married a second husband John Holmes, of Low Craig.

Elizabeth

Thomas

Hannah

Lucy
(d. 1806) married
Westgarth Forster (d. 1797) of Unthank Hall, Durham.†

Lucy
married Thomas Emmerson.

Susannah

John

Sarah

Susannah

George

Westgarth
The Author of "Strata,"
Born; 1772; Died, 1835.

Phœbe
died 1836;
married Thomas Brown who died 1833.

William
died 1812.

Mary
died 1814

* Abstracted chiefly from *The genealogical list of the descendant of Thomas and Elizabeth Brown of Eshgill down to 23rd April, 1790*, in the possession of T. F. Brown, Esq., of Bristol.
† The home of the Westgarths. George Forster had married Mary Westgarth. This Westgarth Forster was their son.

Westgarth Forster was born in 1772 and was the eldest of several children.

His father occupied the post of Manager of the Allendale Mines, and upon his death in 1797, his son was appointed his successor, and continued to hold the post till 1807. He then resigned his occupation as mine agent, and, together with his sister Susan, occupied Ivy House, Garrigill, alternating the duties of a farmer with researches for his book which appeared in 1809.

In 1810 he became mine surveyor, and laboured in his profession with enthusiasm until 1833.

A second edition of his "Strata" appeared in 1821.

During this period his energies led him far beyond the mineral areas of the North. We find him in Wales, distant English counties like Somerset, and also in the mining regions of Spain and America. He met with a measure of financial success, and in his most prosperous days his income ran easily into four figures. But reverses set in, and the closing years of the life of this clever man were saddened by successive losses, caused by what has been called a mania for mining speculations.*

At the "winning of the hay"† in 1833 he walked into Garrigill practically a penniless man.

Repeated misfortune had undermined his health, and he died poor and depressed in spirit.

In 1834 he parted with his plate, pictures, and books, for daily sustenance, and expired at Ivy House as recorded on his tomb stone, Nov. 9th, 1835.

3. THE REV. BLYTHE HURST, M.A., PH. D.

This remarkable man, Curate of Garrigill, 1842—1845, was born July 6th, 1806. He was sent to school when four years of

---

* See W Nall's third edition of Westgarth Forster's *Strata*, p. XLV.

† Vide Appendix F.

IVY HOUSE ("THE HIVIN").

Wallace says it was built in 1790, but it was, in part, standing a hundred years before this. One portion bears the date of 1694.

age, where he learned to read the New Testament, and at seven was sent to work in a smith's shop at Winlaton. As a youth he joined the Wesleyans, and became an acceptable local preacher. When about nineteen he began the pursuit of knowledge under difficulties of the most arduous character. In his daily labour he was employed from six in the morning till eight in the evening. His wages were small, and few books were at his command. Having determined to master the Greek language, and being possessed of one shilling and sixpence, he set off to Newcastle and bought a Greek Grammar at a second hand book stall. Having little time to spare, he wrote the declensions of the nouns, and the conjugations of the verbs, upon the flame stone which hung before the smith's fire to protect his face from the heat, and by this means he got them off by heart. He afterwards purchased a Greek Testament, and, at the age of twenty-one, being in possession of a pound note, he secured a Greek Lexicon. Gradually he became proficient not only in Greek, but in Hebrew and Syriac also.

At about thirty years of age he left the Wesleyan Society, but continued to do the work of a lay-preacher in connection with another Methodist body. In 1840, he wrote a tract, in reply to a socialist lecturer. The Rector of Winlaton sent a copy to the Bishop (Maltby) of Durham, who after reading it, asked the Rector for further particulars of the author's life. Further enquiries led the the Bishop to have an interview with the young blacksmith, the result being that it was arranged that he should undergo the usual examinations, with the view of being ordained as a clergyman of the English Church. Not long after he was appointed as Curate-in-Charge of Garrigill, and resided at Crossgill House, the Parsonage not being built then. He was afterwards Vicar of Slaley, and later of Collierly.

After Mr. Hurst became a clergyman, and had time at his command for study, he became a linguist of the highest order. In addition to his complete acquaintance with the modern European languages, he was master of Hebrew, Syriac, Sanscrit, Chaldaic, Persian, and Arabic. In recognition of his scholarly attainments the degree of PH. D. was conferred on him by the University of Rostock, in Germany.

After a long life of usefulness, he died in 1882, widely acknowledge to be one of the most distinguished men of his day. His remains rest in the cemetery at Winlaton, where a granite tombstone stands to his memory, bearing the inscription :—

> " In affectionate remembrance of the Rev.
> Blythe Hurst, M A , Ph D , Vicar of
> Colherly, in the county of Durham, who
> died June 24, 1882, aged 76 years "

Some of the oldest of our residents have a very vivid remembrance of Blythe Hurst, and were very powerfully impressed at the time of his residence here with the originality and force of his character.[*]

4. JOSEPH SHIELD. The last of the old Parish Clerks in Garrigill died in 1895. The then incumbent thus referred to him in the local Church Magazine :—

"I regret to say our last note this month must refer to a loss which has been sustained not only by the Church, but also by the whole village, by the death of Mr. Joseph Shield, our Parish Clerk and village newsagent. Garrigill has lost one of her notabilities of whom she was justly proud. He passed quietly away at his own house, aged 73, on June 27th, and was buried the following Sunday in the Churchyard. Nearly all the newspapers at Newcastle and Carlisle have given a notice of his death, so we need not repeat here what they say of his connection with the first locomotive, and the positions of trust which he held in

---

* For a fuller record see Bourn, *History of the Parish of Ryton* (1896).

the lead mining industry. He was known best among us as Parish Clerk, and among the elder ones as teacher of the Night School for nearly 20 years. The present generation with all the advantages of state-aided education cannot appreciate the benefits, perhaps, which Mr. Shield's Night School conferred, but their fathers can. We must remember that to come in tired from work and sit down to teach a lot of lads involved self-sacrifice on the part of their old master. As a singer too, he was well known; in his day he was perhaps the best for many miles round, and old people even now remember the beauty of the music he used to produce when he went up the hill sides practising. His loss will be most felt by the Church, where for 44 years he transacted the duties of Parish Clerk. His funeral sermon was preached from the text, Psalm lxxxiv. 10., when the preacher gave voice to the sympathy felt by the congregation for his widow and children, and to the loss the absence of his voice and presence would be in their services."

The year 1900 was one of great sorrow in Garrigill.

Death succeeded death until we were appalled, especially, as in many cases, those who fell were very prominent in our village life.

The following is part of a list, which I published at Christmas 1900, of those who had passed away during the previous year, or a little more :—

Joseph Watson	...	79
John Curragh	...	56
James Vipond	...	68
Thomas Hornsby Todd		27
Sarah J. Bramwell	...	24
Adam Pickering	...	72
Annie Armstrong	...	31
Henry Millican		66
John Elliott		72
Annie Hall	...	55
Edward Raine	...	76
John Archer	...	51
Joseph Vipond	...	68
Arthur Dobson	. .	64

With the exception of four of these they were all, in different ways, and according to their ability, stalwart supporters of the Church. Some were never absent from the Sunday Services except through sickness. Many congregations, even in large town populations, would stagger under such a blow as is here indicated. We are glad to say that the Church in Garrigill not only stood firm, but gathered strength.

Never were the average congregations better. The offerings surpassed every previous record in the history of our work.

In more recent times the community has been impoverished by the death of such men as James Moffat, George Pickering, John Shield (son of the Parish Clerk), Jonathan Greenwell, the brothers Walton, and the brothers Thomas and John Hodgson, also James Vipond, Junior.

CHAPTER XIX.

NATHANAEL BURNAND—CALAMY'S ACCOUNT—THE COTTAGE CHAPEL —JOHN DAVY—REGINALD WALTON —BITTER STRIFE—REDWING— SUCCESSIVE PREACHERS— THE METHODISTS.

It is said that Dissent was introduced into Garrigill by Nathanael Burnand, Presbyterian, who held the living of Brampton, under The Commonwealth. He was compelled to surrender the Vicarage by the Act of Uniformity in 1662.*

The following is Calamy's account of Burnand :—

"Brampton, Mr. Burnand. He was the son of old Mr. Nathanael Burnand, the chief minister in Durham in the time of the Civil War. He was bred in Cam-

---

* Vide Appendix G

bridge. When he removed from thence he dwelt three years in the family of Mr. Harrison, of Allecthorp, performing family duties, &c. He was afterwards a noted preacher in this county [Cumberland] till the Bartholomew Act silenced him.* When he was rejected he retired to the 'Desert Places' in *Austin More* and there took a farm and manag'd it carefully in order to obtain a subsistence for his family, preaching in his own house on the Lord's Day to any poor Christians that would come to hear him, and in process of time he preach'd at *Bureston* in public no one taking notice of him. At length, Providence favouring Sir Wm. Blackett in his lead mines, he fixed him there to preach to his miners with an allowance of £30 per ann. He had great success among these ignorant creatures, and did much good. But when the mines fail'd poor Mr. Burnand was again at a loss; came up to London and spent some time with a congregation at

---

* The Act of Uniformity received royal assent May 19th, and became operative on St. Bartholomew's Day, August 24th.

Harwich. But, age coming upon him, he at length came to London again and subsisted upon the charity of well-disposed Christians till death gave him his *Quietus.*"[*]

Calamy's phrase "desert places in Austin More" refers to Garrigill.

The first home of the Presbyterians whom Burnand gathered around him still stands—a small cottage on the left of the "lonning [†]" which ascends from Bridge End, now known as Loaning Head. It is, however, extremely doubtful if this were Burnand's "own house" in Calamy's story. It was no doubt erected as a Chapel after the Toleration Act of 1689.[‡]

This account of the introduction of Dissent must be modified. Burnand receiv-

---

[*] Calamy, Account of the Ejected and Silenc'd Ministers, Vol II, p 158.

[†] Lonnin or Lonning, a lane.

[‡] When this Chapel was abandoned it became first a mine shop, then a meeting house for the Methodists, and subsequently a cottage, and so remains.

ed his licence on September the 5th, 1672. But, more than two months before this, John Davy, a Congregationalist, obtained a licence to preach in Garrigill (June 20th, 1672) in the house of Reginald Walton.† Further, Burnand's licence was only a general licence to preach. John Davy, therefore, was really the pioneer of Dissent in this valley.

The name of Reginald Walton, in whose house Davy preached, is somewhat strangely associated with the Church in Garrigill.

During the restoration when the Rev. P. T. Lee, M.A., was Curate-in-Charge, a monumental slab, lying in the Church-yard, was brought into the Church for its better preservation, because it is inscribed with a Latin epitaph. It forms part of the Church pavement, but is

---

* Vide *Domestic State Papers*, under this date. Burnand is called Burnam. The page is also wrong in the Calendar Index. Read 574 for 575.

† Vide p 97 and p. 167.

covered with a mat.* It reads as follows :

HIC   IACET   CORPVS   REG
INALD   WALTON   NVP
ER   DE   VPPER   LEEHOVSE
QVI   OBIJT   PRIMO   DIE
AVGVSTI   ANNO   DOMI.
1713   AETATIS   SVEE   93.

Here is a little *mason* Latin. The
mason in cutting the letters has made a
mistake—SVEE should be SVAE. Having
made this correction, the translation
runs :—"Here lies the body of Reginald
Walton, late of Upper Lee-house, who
died on the 1st day of August, in the
year of the Lord 1713, in the 93rd
year of his age."†

It is certainly remarkable that the
tombstone of the first permanently resid-

* Vide *Garrigill Register*, preface (1699-1730).

† There is another memorial stone in the Church,
but it is compartively of recent erection. It relates
to the Little family of Alston.

ent dissenter lies just within the Church door.

In reading over the old records of Garrigill one elevating fact impresses itself upon the mind—the unitedness of the people. In all matters of the Church (which always stood first), the poor, the roads, the constable's affairs, &c., they had only one mind and one way.

I have often been reminded of Macaulay's description of the Roman people in their early days.

> "Then was none for party,
> Then were all for the state.
> Then the rich man helped the poor
> And the poor man loved the great"

In its miniature life this was true of Garrigill in the olden time.

From the advent of Davey and Burnand a change comes over the scene. Prejudices arise, and divided interests manifest themselves. Men elected as Churchwardens refuse to serve. Parents register their children but refuse to have

O

them baptized, and so forth. The disciples of the dissenting preachers far outran their teachers, and the clamorous voices of bitter strife distracted this once harmonious valley.

Matters became so bad as to find a permanent place in our public records.

The following is taken from The State Papers in the Rolls Office :—

"Feb 9, 1676/7.

"John Walton and others, for speaking against the Church of England

"Before Sir Philip Musgrave, Bart Thomas Walton of Aldstone Moor, Gent , Saith that being in company of Lionell Walton of the Bridge End, his son John Walton, and others, and discoursing about a Minister Mr Burnard,* who related to this informer some discourse that passed between himself and one John Walton of Gatehead concerning the Church of England, which Church Mr Bernard held to be a true Church . the said John Walton denied it. The Company now present said they thought that John Walton was in the right. They did also endeavour to prove by arguments that the Church of England was a false Church, viz ·—The King is a foresworn man, then how

---

* For Burnand Also spelt Burnam. See p. 191.

could he establish a true Church? . . . . They did also affirm that the Church of England was going on the broad way to destruction They also said that if the Church of England went to heaven, hell would be very empty. They also affirmed, and took in hand to prove, that those that used the Book of Common Prayer would be damned They endeavoured to prove it out of some text in Collossians II. 21-22 "

Oh the pity of it!—that a once united people—a tiny community too— should be made, in the name of religion, enemies to one another We must, however, forgive all this, for among all parties alike, these were days when men had no idea of tolerance.

In 1749 the farm at Red Wing was purchased as an endowment for dissenting preaching and worship, and a chapel was erected there. The date on the headstone of the door is 1756 ·· This "Cause" passed into the hands of the Congregationalists, and so remains at this day, the Presbyterians having .disappeared †

---

* Wallace wrongly says it was built in 1754

† Many of the congregations founded by the Presbyterians have become " Independent " and many of them " Unitarian."

The congregation left by Mr. Burnand
secured the services of a Mr. Thomas
Dawes.* *The Congregational Magazine*
for 1822 informs us that by the will of
Nathanael Burnand dated 1703, the interest
of £30 was to be given yearly to his
successors in office, who should preach
in the Garrigill Meeting-house. His books
were included in the same bequest.
These last were to be lent also to
different members of the congregation.
The next pastor was called Turner, and
he, on his removal to Berwick-upon-
Tweed, was succeeded by Dickinson, who
afterwards went to Fisher Street, Carlisle.
Then came Adam Wilson, who preached
alternately for twenty years at Garrigill
and Irshope Burn. After him we find
the name of James Richie, M.D, who
after labouring for twelve years at Garrigill, about the year 1751, took charge of
a congregation at Plumpton, in conjunc-
tion with Garrigill. He seems, however,

---

* The following items were collected by a predecessor of mine at Garrigill, and printed in the local
magazine.

THE ENTRANCE TO REDWING PREACHING HOUSE.

Opp. p. 196.

to have found this too much for him, for very shortly afterwards he left the region of the Helm Wind[*] and went to Yorkshire, Thomas Smith taking his place at Garrigill. During the residence of Smith, the meeting-house was removed from Loaning Head to a new building which had been erected about the year 1756, at Redwing, and which still stands. The next Minister was Mr. John Dean, who remained here three years, and then removed to North Shields. In the year 1763, Mr. Timothy Nelson, of Penruddock, was invited to take charge of Garrigill, where he continued till 1800, when he resigned, and returned to his native place. *The Congregational Magazine* goes on to tell us that "When Mr. Nelson left Garrigill the cause had almost dwindled away, and would in all probability have been entirely lost, had it not been for the disinterested, and benevolent exertions of Mr. John Dickinson, of Alston, who was formerly of Garrigill. He took a

---

[*] For a good account of The Helm Wind, see Sopwith, *Alston Moor*, 58-63.

lively concern in the declining cause, and
engaged Mr. Wm. Norris, Senior, to preach
in Alston and the neighbourhood. Under
Mr. Norris a Church was formed at
Alston, and received into union with
itself the remains of the old Church at
Garrigill. The meeting-house at Alston
was erected in the year 1804."* To day

---

* The following is from a letter by Mr Wm
Norris.—"After the removal of Mr. Nelson from
Garrigill, I think in 1803, I received a very pressing
invitation to visit Alston Moor, which I complied with
from no futher design than an itinerant excursion for
a fortnight, during which interval I preached at
Garrigill, Alston Town, and several adjacent places;
the result of which visit was an Independent interest
raised at Alston, and a student from Hoxton Academy
was engaged to supply them, but not liking the
country he staid but a short time there, and on his
leaving them they applied to me again, requesting
that I would go and take the pastoral charge of the
newly-raised congregation in connection with the
vacancy at Garrigill. This, after earnest prayer, much
deliberation, and the advice of candid, disinterested
friends I complied with. For some time we carried
on regular worship at Alston in the room of an inn
but the use of a more convenient apartment at a
spinning manufactory being offered us by a friend, we
removed to it, and continued to preach three times
every Lord's day, and one evening in the week, until
the encouraging prospects of religious matters induc-

there is no regular congregation at Garrigill
but the minister at Alston takes an occasional service at Red Wing Chapel.†

It has been noticed that the Independent cause, after flourishing in Garrigill for about a hundred years, meets
with a check during the latter half of
the xviii century, which brings it to the
verge of entire destruction. One cause
of this was the rise of a new factor in
the religious life of the chapelry.‡ The
religious revival in the Church of England
during this period made itself felt almost
immediately in our remote valley. On
Thursday, 28th July 1748, that great
Churchman, the Rev. John Wesley, came
riding over the moor to Nenthead, where

---

ed us to erect a chapel, which, together with the
burying ground, is vested in the hands of trustees,
according to the usual mode of Independent churches
The whole of the ground was given by Mr. William
Todd, about half the expense for building the Chapel
was raised by the friends at Alston, and the remainder
I got in London, including a small sum which I
collected among my friends in Yorkshire and Durham."

† Vide Appendix J on Renwick.

‡ Vide p 91.

he preached at eight o'clock. Four hours later, he addressed a " quiet staring people " at Alston Cross who seemed to be little concerned one way or the other. Garrigill, as far as I can learn, he passed by without a visit But nevertheless, the inhabitants, not long after, formed a "society." In 1765 this Society used to meet in the house at Loaning Head, which the followers of Burnand had vacated when they moved to Red Wing. In 1778 a resident Methodist preacher was appointed to Alston, and some time about the year 1790, a Chapel was built at Low Houses, Garrigill. This Chapel was "restored," several times and in 1859 it was rebuilt.

In 1825 a chapel was built in Garrigill belonging to another Methodist body—the Primitive Methodists. The present chapel bears the date 1885. To-day, there are not less than six preaching houses in the Garrigill area.

APPENDICES.

APPENDIX A.
"Sir" as applied to a priest.
See p 26 and p. 37.

The first priest responsible for the ecclesiastical duties of Garrigill, so far as we have been able to recover the names of the clergy, bore the title "Sir."

It must not be supposed that this designation represented any dignity, on the part of the priest, apart from his office in the Church.

Anciently this title was the common designation of the parson of a parish.

There is an instance of this use in *Archaeologia Aeliana* third series, vol. ii. It is specially interesting because of the date, and also the locality. It is given in a memorandum among the papers of Colonel Gascoigne, Leeds, relating to purchases at Corbridge Fair, Northumberland, in 1298. The time and place approximate to the circumstances of the negligent Parson of Alston-cum-Garrigill.

The entry runs :—" De Domino Willelmo, Capellano, iiij boves, precium bovis ixs. De eodem domino Willelmo, Capellano, v boves, precium bovis vjs viij."

Translation —

Of Sir William, the chaplain, 4 ox, price per

ox 9s. Of the same Sir William, the chaplain, 5 ox, price per ox, 6s 8d.

The occurrence of the title in Shakspeare is well-known.

As you like it   Act iii, Sc 3.—

" *Touchstone*. Here comes Sir Oliver   Sir Oliver you are well met   Will you dispatch us here under this tree, or shall we go with you to your chapel ? "

Merry wives Act ii, Sc 1 —

" *Shallow :* Sir, there's a fray to be fought between Sir Hugh the Welsh priest and Caius the French doctor."

Similarly we have Sir Topas in *Twelfth Night*, and Sir Nathanael in *Love's Labour Lost, &c.*

It is easy to see how the designation passed into general use at a period when the Three Estates of the Realm—The Clergy, the Lords Temporal, and the Commons—were sharply defined * In Tudor days, it has been said, the term was somewhat loosely used to connote a University degree.

There have been a few cases of harmless pedantry, in which men have tried to maintain the title, in modern times

---

* Constitutional England began in 1295 when the Three Estates met for administration in one " House."

APPENDIX B.

Gaingill Font.

See page 70.

When the old font was re-erected in 1899 the event was held up to ridicule in the *Methodist Recorder* by a writer known as H K * in that paper.

I desire not to say or write one word which would not conduce to love and peace among Christian men, but in the interests of truth I am compelled to state this case.

The following is, in part, what appeared in the *Methodist Recorder* —

"A comical mishap befell the curate-in-charge a few months ago. One day, like Mr Pickwick, his zeal for antiquities was rewarded by the discovery of an "ancient font" He rescued it from oblivion, restored it, exalting it upon a stone pedestal, and replanted it in the Church He then issued a circular with a bishop's mitre in the corner, and "matins" and "evensong" displayed in stately style—all eminently correct. He informed his parishioners, who informed the world at large, of the discovery of the ancient font in which "the rude forefathers of the hamlet" were baptised, and announced solemn services of reconsecration This circular fell into the hands of an ancient Methodist, who informed her friends that the parson was all wrong. Her own brother (the village

---

* Nehemiah Curnock, Wesleyan Minister.

clerk) fifty years ago, taking compassion on the then
fontless condition of the little Church in Garrigill,
unearthed a huge boulder stone of suitable shape and
hewed it into a font, mounting it upon a wooden
stand.

" It was used for a long time, until, perhaps
because the pedestal was supposed to be unsafe or
unsightly, it fell into disuse and was left lying about
in neglect   The Parson did his level best in a local
newspaper to maintain the pure unadulterated antiquity
of his font

" But the good women, who herself showed me
the circular, says that she knows her brother, who
was a mason, hewed out the font from a boulder
with his own hands."

The article contains many personalities, which I
do not characterize, and which (for the sake of christian
sentiment) I omit.

The above paragraphs, from the *Methodist Recorder*,
are false down to the tiniest particulars. *They do not
contain one line of truth from beginning to end.*

1.—It is not true that I professed to discover
an ancient font.   The ancient font was never lost.
It was carefully preserved and handed on from one
Clergyman to another.

2 —It is not true that I did my "level best
in a local newspaper to maintain the pure unadulterated antiquity of the font."   I never wrote about the font
to any local paper, nor any paper whatever, nor did
anyone else with my knowledge and permission   Two
paragraphs attacking my circular, and quoting the

"good woman" to whom the Editor of the *Methodist Recorder* refers appeared in the local press, but of these I took no notice.

3—IT IS NOT TRUE that the Church was fontless. I have turned up two orders by the Archdeacon of Northumberland, dated respectively July 1763, and October 1768.

In the former he orders a "new cover for the font" (p. 128). This was a wooden lid or tabernacle for the stone font

On the second occasion the order runs .—

"That a bason for the font be provided" (p 131) This was an inside vessel to stand in the bowl of the font. The font was not perforated at the base It was still *in this state* when it came into my hands. The perforation was done at its re-erection in 1899.

4 —IT IS NOT TRUE that the Clerk was a mason. Singularly enough, in my search, in corners likely and unlikely, for information, I met with documentary information about the employment of Mr Thomas Peart. An old wage book belonging to a Garrigill mine came into my hands. There, Thomas Peart appears as a *miner*. This has led me to make further investigations, and I now can prove that the once clerk was by turn a miner, a policeman, an employé in a glass works, etc., but *never a mason*. As the fact that the clerk was supposed to be a mason was one of the strong points of the attack referred to, it is only fair that the truth should be stated I write this note without predjudice of any kind, and solely in the interest of the history of our fabric

5 —IT IS NOT TRUE that the font in question "fell into disuse" because "the pedestal was unsafe or unsightly," and was left "lying about in neglect."

The whole suggestion is absolutely fictitious The gentleman who was responsible for its removal still lives to give his own explanation (p 68)

He passed over the local stone being enamoured with the one which had done duty in the mother Church

6 —IT IS NOT TRUE that a *re-consecration* service was held, and the description of the circular is false in more than one particular A copy of the paper lies before me as I write

What is the only verdict that must be given by an honest mind upon such a closely woven tissue of mistatements ?

In the Market Place at Alston a good Methodist, expressing his opinion of the *Methodist Recorder* article, said, "It's not matterable ! It's all babblement, and tarrable stuffment !" I am persuaded that this is, after all, the best way in which to regard this attack Well, now let us look at the theory of H. K as to the Garrigill Font He asks us to accept the statement, that about fifty years ago a certain man "unearthed a huge boulder stone of suitable shape and hewed it into a font" Against this, I urge the affidavit which contains the statements of the Revd. Octavius James, and the Rev. George Monkhouse (p 68), Curates-in-charge of Garrigill H. K. says the "mason's" sister was his informant Is it fair to write a thing down on the verbal testimony of one person, and that person advanced in years, without any scrap of evidence. especially when the testimony is a mere reminiscence of half-a-century ago, and given by one who is, rightly and naturally so, an interested party—the sister of the "mason" It has never been denied that the "mason" had something to do with the present state of the font. The story in Chapter XI admits that he had. It will be seen that the "cleaning" of the font was mistaken for its "making" For the facts the reader is referred to the account there given I know of a still stranger story than that of Garrigill Font—a case in which a captured Church font has been erected in a *Methodist Chapel* !

APPENDIX C
The will of Catherine Emmerson.
See page 151

The will of Catherine Emmerson of Esh* -gill gives a pleasing glimpse into the comfort of the Garrigill homes two hundred years ago. The will was signed May 30th, 1712. The testatrix was buried June 4th, 1712

The will was printed in *The Newcastle Magazine* in 1826.

" In the name of God   Amen. I Kathern Emerson, of Eshgill, in the Chapelry of Garrigill, Diocese of Durham, being sick of body, but of good and perfect remembrance (Blessed be God for the same) calling to mind the uncertainty of this mortal life, do make and ordain this my last will and testament, in manner and form following .—

First, and principally, I commit my soul into the hands of God, my Creator, hoping assuredly, through the merits of Christ Jesus, my Redeemer, to obtain full and free remission of all my sins ; and my body to the earth of which it is made, to be buried in the Chapel or Chapellyard of Garragill, at the discretion of my executors hereafter named; and as for those temporal goods which the Lord has been pleased to bestow upon me I give, and bequeath them, as followeth :—

*Esh, A S Ash, Fraximus Excelsior.

Itm. I give unto my cousin Hannah, the daughter of Thomas Dickinson, one reed Rugg, one chest of Drawers, one Feather Bed, one pair of Curtains, my best Kettlell, one Trunk, thire of my best Pewter Dishes, half-dozen best Trenchers, one-dozen Spoons, one diaper Table Cloth, with one-dozen diaper Napkins, one Pewther Tanket, one pair of best Blankets, and one pair of Sheets of the best, and two best Bolsters, and one Happin,* one Iron Girdell, and the best Brass Pan, three Plates, and a Brass Candestick, and a Frying Pan, and a Diessei, and a Press, a Table, and Brandith †

Itm. I give unto Kathern, the daughter of Arthur Emeison, a Feather Bed, one green Rugg, one pair of green Curtains, one pair of Blankets, and a pair of Sheets, and a Bolster, two Pewter Dishes, half-a-dozen of Trenchers, and six Spoons, one Pewter Tankard, a Kettell, and half-a-dozen Napkins, a candlestick, and a Bason.

Itm I give to Ann, daughter of Matthew Batson ‡ one Hapin, two Blankets, two Sheets, one Bolster, six Napkins, one Kettell, one Tanket, two Pewter Dishes, and a Candlestick.

Itm. I give Mary Richardson, daughter to Caleb Richardson, two Happins, two Blanketts, and two Sheets, one Boulster, and two Pewter Dishes.

---

* A thick woven bedcover.

† Brandreth, an iron frame for suspending the girdle, or baking plate, above the fire

‡ Matthew Bateson lived at Dodberry He had just buried his daughter Jane

Itm. I give my four friends at Newcastle, to each of them, the sum of Twenty Shillings, and my common wearing Cloths, to be equally divided amongst them.

Itm. I give to Isabell Walton one dress of Head Close, a Manty, and a Petty Coate.

Itm. I give to Lucy Holmes Ten Shillings

Itm I give to Elizabeth Archer One Pound.

Itm I give Thomas Browne Ten Shillings.

Itm. I give Mary Wallass Ten Shillings.

Itm I give Ann Bailes Five Shillings

Itm. I give Thomas Dickinson, Josh Dickinson, Mattw Batson, and Caleb Richardson—each of them Ten Shillings

Itm. I give to Hannah Dickinson a Brewing Tub, three Barrels, two Stands, twelve Bottles, and two Skeels,* a Possett-pot,† and a pair of Temps ‡

Itm. I give Mary Dickinson twelve Bottles

Itm I give Isabel Emerson, Kathern Ritson, and Abigill Batson, all the rest of my Bottles, equally to be divided amongst them

Itm. I give to Thomas Dickinson a Gunn and a Bybell.

---

*Skeel, a large water tub.

† Poss, to be saturated It is applied to a thick hot drink, and also to treading or beating wet clothes. In the latter case a poss-tub is used

‡ Tems, a hair sieve

Itm. I give to the poor of Garragill Two Pounds, the interest to be paid at first Martinmas after my death, and so to continue.*

Itm. I give to Joseph Dickinson one Pot, one Yetling,† one Crook and Tongs, and three Skeels and two Pocks.

Itm I give to Elizabeth Browne, widow, Fifteen Shillings.

Itm. I give to Nicholas Emmerson one Bedstead, one Table, and two Forms

Itm. I give to Arthur Emmerson Fifteen Pounds.

Itm. I give to Elizabeth Batson daughter of Matthew Batson Two Pounds

Itm. I give to Joseph Dickinson one cubbert,‡ one table, one cheese flenck, and a cheese press.

And my will is, that all and every of these legacies mentioned in this, my last will and testament be paid and discharged to the several parties above said, within the space of twelve months, after my death. And I do hereby make Robert Dickinson full and sole executor of this my last will and testament, revoking and disallowing all other wills, by me, at any time heretofore formerly made, and declaring this to be my last will and testament, in witness thereof I have hereunto set my hand and seal, this 30th, day of May Anno Domini 1712. It is further agreed before the signing of this will, that if the said

---

* See p 151.　† Yetling, a pan with a bow　‡ For cupboard

within Robert Dickinson should happen to dye before he comes to the age of twenty-one years, that then I make Joseph Dickinson, son of Thomas Dickinson, to be my executor. Sealed, signed, and delivered in the presence of us,

> Gilbert Walton.
> John Archer.*
> *Kathern Emmerson.*"

---

* See the Archer pedigree, p. 163.

APPENDIX D.
The Paine Roll.
See page 165.

The word Paine is a form of the word penalty. It is derived from the French, *Peine,* or the Latin *Poena.*

In the Paine Roll of Alston penalties are attached for breach of the regulations made by the Bye-law Court of the Manor with the approval of the inhabit-ants.

The Roll appears to have been revised in 1597, 1629, and 1692 and the Drift Roll again in 1744 as the following lists show :—

List of the Juries empaneled at the copying of the Paine and Drift Rolls of Alston :—

1597.

A Paine Roll agreed upon by the Jury hereunder written with the likeing and advice of Thomas Hilton Esquire, Lord of the Manor and Wm Hutton Esq., Steward together with the consent and agreement of the whole Lordship, 5 Oct. 39 Elizabeth and drawn forth of *a Roll made in King Henry VII days* *

---

* Henry VII 1485-1509

Thomas Yeats of Fairhill
Thomas Walton of Newshield.
John Walton of Raise
John Eales.
Thomas Hutchinson
George Lee of the Cragge.
Thomas Crozier.
Nicholas Walton of Galligill
John Bowman
Nicholas Walton of Blackhouse.
Nicholas Richerson.
Alexander Walton
Richard Teasdale

PAINE ROLL
1629

Andrew Teasdale
Richard Walton of Lee House.
Henry Renwick.
Christopher Harrison.
Henry Hutchinson
Arthur Lee
Thomas Nixon.
Reginald Nixon.
Richard Vipond of Nent Hall.
John Walton of Natterasse.
Thomas Stephenson.
Lionell Dickinson
John Teasdale

PAINE ROLL
1692.

Thomas Vipond, *Foreman.*
Nicholas Whitfield.

Thomas Watson
Henry Stephenson
Robert Archer.
Ralph Whitfield
Nathaniel Walton
John Dickinson.
John Lee.
Thomas Walton.
John Smith
John Walton.
William Lee.

There are two lists for 1744, which do not agree.

Two items may be selected to illustrate the nature of the Paine Roll.

1 —"*That the Butts of Alston and Garrigill be yearly made before St. Helen's Day upon Payne of 3 shillings and 4 pence for every default*" The Garrigill Butts are shown on p 172

2.—A relic of the New Year's Saturnalia appears in another law "*That no man play at cards on tables, for money, within the Lordship, but within the twelve days of Christmas sub pena 6s 8d toties quoties*"

The Paine Roll was published in *The Cumberland and Westmorland Advertiser* (Penrith) in February 1892.

The Drift Roll refers to the driving of the sheep upon the Fells, etc The Drift Roll has not been published, I think.

APPENDIX E.

Census of 1824.

See page 168.

An account of the number of the inhabitants of the Chapelry of Garrigill taken in the year 1824, by Thomas Shaw of Shield Hill:—

Jno. Archer and Family	12
Ralph Stephenson	8
Alboracy (*sic*) Bell	11
Margrate Parmley	8
Jno Bell	5
Jno. Roa	7
Israil Noals	7
Jos Winskil	5
Thos Modeland	6
Isabella Winskill	4
Robt Eliot	5
Jno. Archer, Junr.	5
Jno Lankistor	7
Geo Spark	6
Wm Thomonson	5
Jos Pattinson	3
Jos Wandliss	4
Adam Walton	3
Richd Thomonson	7
Isaac Teasdale	5
Hannah Bell	6
Isaac Winskil	4
Wm Dent	7

Mary Bell	1
Wm. Coats	2
Hugh Pickering	9
Nancy Rain	6
Isaac Bell	4
Joshua Johnston	6
Sarah Whitfield	5
Do Do. Lodgers	3
Joseph Vartie	10
Leand Shield	2
John Race	3
Jno. Pearson	5
Thos. Shield	6
Eliz. Hetherington	5
Eliz. Noals	5
Wm. Vipond	3
Thos Vipond	4
Jos Vipond, Junr.	3
Thos. Bowman	2
Hugh Spark	9
Jos. Vipond, Senr.	4
Jno. Trumel	11
Jno Vipond	2
Jno. Wallace	7
Jos Hall	5
Isaac Hornsby	6
Jane Parmly	5
Robt Pearson	5
Jos. Currah	3
Jos. Shield	8
Jno. Proud	4
Jno. Watson	7
Jos. Renwick	7
Mary Renwick	2
Sarah Richardson	5

Huntei Ward	... ...	7
Henry Renwick	...	6
Jno Coats	... ...	2
James Dickinson	...	7
Jno Watson	... ...	9
Anthony Siddle	...	6
Thos Armstrong	... ...	7
Jos. Elliot	...	8
Henry Cragg	... ...	3
Mary Currah	...	5
Jos Hetherington	... ...	8
Benjaman Wallace	...	8
Robt. Hodgson	.. ..	5
Mary Coats	...	6
Mary Ward	...	3
Jos Richardson	...	3
Eliz Horsley	... .	4
Thos Kidd	...	5
Jos Slack	... ...	4
Jno Hodgson	...	10
Jos. Lowes	... ...	6
Jos. Beastin	.	10
Thos. Archer	... ...	10
Wm. Townson	...	4
Thos. Holms	... ..	5
Jno Holms	...	3
Jno. Teasdale	... ...	5
Isaac Teasdale	...	2
Hannah Dickinson	...	4
Thos. Peart	...	3
Matthew Hill	... ...	4
Thos. Hall	...	7
Phillas Davinson	... ...	6
Tachous Holms	...	8
Jane White	... ...	2

Jos Teasdale	...	3
Thos. Medcalf	...	10
Jno Teasdale	...	5
Thos. Bell	...	3
Adam Elliot	...	5
Jno. Davinson	...	4
Jonathan Davinson	...	9
Robt Davinson	...	4
Joshua Bell	...	2
Nancy Cousin	...	6
Robt. Simpson	...	5
Umphra Maddinson	...	3
Thos Coulthard	...	6
Matthew Watson	...	5
Jane Hetherington	.	6
Jno. Smith	...	8
Wm Gill's widdow	..	6
Wm Graham	.	5
Jos. Pattinson	..	6
Robt. Parker	...	5
Geo Smith	..	7
Thos Harrison	...	10
Thos. Pickering	...	10
Geo Wilkinson	...	4
Thos Walton	...	10
Thos. Watson	...	9
Hannah Gray	...	4
Leckle Craig	...	10
Jno. Vipond	...	9
Peter Bainbridge	...	7
Jos. Stephenson	..	8
Thos Teasdale	...	2
Thos. Shaw	...	7
Jno. Couper	...	2
James Robinson	...	6

Jos Teasdale	... ...	9
Wilkinson Smith	...	10
Robinson Allinson ...	...	4
Wm. Longstaf	...	5
John Atkinson	... ...	6
Isaac Craig	...	6
Ralph Winskil	... ...	10
Mary Teasdale	. .	5
Jno. Peart	... ...	2
Wm. Peart	...	5
Robt. Shaw	... ...	2
Jno. Jakes	...	4
Wm. Herdman	... ...	4
Betty Wallace	...	4
Friend Wallace	... ...	4
Jos Wallace	...	5
Hannah Bell	... ...	3
Jacob Peart	...	4
Wm. Heslop	... ...	3
Nancey Hetherton	...	7
Enock Noals	... ...	4
Wm. Craig	...	4
Isaac Gill	... ...	5
Wm. Gill	...	5
Nancey Pickring	... ...	4
Geo Swindale	...	10
Hannah Pearson	... ...	2
James Teasdale	...	6
Jos. Teasdale	. . ...	9
Isaac Teasdale	..	9
Thos Todd	... ...	8
Wm Armstrong	...	8
Jackson Wandlis	... ...	4
Ralph Armstrong	...	12
Thos. Atkinson	... ...	3

Hannah Watson	...		5
Thos. Pearson	...	...	2
Wm. Kidd		...	4
Jno. Pearson	...	...	7
Thos. Pearson, Jnr.		...	3
Peggy Dobson	...	...	6
Jno. Millican		...	6
Thos. Smith	...	...	9
James Millican		...	5
Jos. Currah	...	...	7
Sarah Lows		...	6
Jno. Craig	...	...	6
Guy Allinson		...	2
Mary Parker	...	...	9
Nancey Lee		...	7
Jos. Craig	...	...	8
Jos. Hutchinson		...	12
Jonathan Lee	...	...	4
Wm. Slack...		...	5
Stephen Watson	...	...	5
Isaac Vipond		...	2
Jason Stephenson ...		...	8
Thomas Millican		...	9
Peter Waugh	...	...	9
Thos. Millican		...	7
Wm. Watson	...	...	8
Wm. Slack		...	5
Jno. Allison	...	...	4
Jno. Slack...		...	8
Jno. Watson	...	...	9
Jno. Currah...		...	3
Thos. Currah	...	...	5
Eliz. Henderson		...	7
Mary Dawson	...	...	2
Jno. Dodd...		...	3

Thos Wallace ...	...	2
Wm. Thomason	...	2
Joshua Bateson ..	• ...	4
Jno. Dawson	...	3
Cuthbert Rodham .	.	6
Hannah Little	...	5
Jno Peart ...	. .	5
Wm Bird ...	...	3
Jos. Lankister ..	...	2
Thos Vipond	. .	4
Wm. Burbeck ...	...	5
Malby Modeland	...	6
Thos Dawson ..	...	6
Geo. Peart...	...	5
Thos Grinwill ...	...	5
Mary Hodgson	...	4
Jno. Stout, Senr ..	. .	4
Jno Cleminson	. .	9
James Vipond ...	..	3
Jos. Spark. .	...	7
Lewcey Dobson ..	...	3
Hannah Gill ..	...	6
James Mulcastor ...	...	10
Geo. Pickring	...	3
Jno. Dobson ...	...	7
Thos Brown	...	6
Rebeckah Lankistor	...	2
Hannah Vipond	...	4
Wm. Stout ...	...	2
Ann Spark...	...	1
Robt. Pearson ...	...	2
Thos. Dawson, jun.	...	2
Jos. Ritson ...	...	3
Jno. Thomonos	...	6
Jno. Stout, jun, ...	...	4

Jos Little		9
Jno Bowman		6
Jno. Bell ... -		7
Jos Bradwell		1
Jno Ritson ..		9
Henry Wilkinson		7
Mary Plets ...		3
Jno Watson		3
Nancey Bateson		4
Jno Elliot		8
Wm Elliot ...		7
Sarah Couper		1
Jno Vipond ...		9
Jno Shield		5
Mary Morah ..		8
Mark Armstrong		6
Edwd Parinly .		9
Thos Parmly		9
Thos White ...		9
Jno Colthard		6
Thos Vipond ...		6
Thos. Wails		9
Wm. Parmley ...		4
Wm Moffat		9
Agniss Moffit ...		8
Isable Watson		8
Wm. Lows ...		8
Isaac Vipond		8
Abraham Watson ...		3
James Bell		4
Jno Vipond ...		8
Nancy Milburn		3
Thos Vipond ...		6
Jane Whitfield		6
Jno. Rain ...		8

Isaac Watson	...		...	6
Jonathan Spark		...		9
Jacob Watson	...		...	7
Joseph Watson		...		6
Sarah Watson	...		...	7
Abraham Watson		...		4
Wm Tomlinson	...		...	4

Total number...   ...   1540

APPENDIX. F.
" Winning of the Hay."
See page 180.

When I first went to the North, a word connected
with the harvest particularly arrested my attention.
One was familiar with it through the ballad of *The
Battle of Otterbourne*—the " winning of the hay."

> "Yt felle abowght the Lammas tyde,
> Whan husbonds wynn ther haye,
> The dowghtye Dowglasse bowynd hym to ryde,
> In Ynglond, to take a praye."

But I had never heard it in every day use, and I had
never fully realized its meaning.

The people of the south always speak of " hay-
making."

This difference of terminology indicates a very real
fact.

Amid the Fells, men " win " their hay—snatch it
from the fickle and tempestuous elements. But in the
warmer south the hay is not rescued from un-
friendly weather. There the hay is leisurely made
while the sun generously shines throughout the season.

But the hay time is wonderfully propitious among
the hills sometimes. There have been summers when
the hay, with the best conditions of sun and wind,
has seemed " to make itself."

I have seen a heavy crop cut in the morning,
and put in the barn by the evening of the following
day—in colour a tinted green—stiffly rustling as it
was moved—with a scent outdoing a garden of roses.

Q

APPENDIX G.

Enforced retirement of non-conforming Ministers.
See page 188.

It is a matter of necessity to refer to a question of policy involved in this record. The "expulsion of 2,000 Clergymen from their livings" by the Act of Uniformity in 1662 is very often spoken of as an intolerable wrong This is not a case for appeal to sentiment. It is needful that due respect be paid to the plain facts of the case. Who were the "ejected ministers"? Judged by the Prayer Book, the Canons, and Government of the Church the majority were not Churchmen at all.

Most of them were void of all pretences to ordination of any sort. Many of them were notoriously ignorant. Some of them were foreign and fanatical sectaries, from the Continent. They had seized, without any right, during the anarchy and chaos of the Civil War and Commonwealth, the various benefices in possession of which they were found, at the Restoration of the Monarchy and the Church in 1660.

There are other facts which should be remembered in connection with these affairs.

From 1660 (The Restoration) to 1662 (The Act of Uniformity) many hundreds of these Puritan preachers, some of them not equal to the average mechanic of to-day in qualifications, were allowed to retain the livings to which they had been illegally presented.

Then they were offered Episcopal ordination, if they would use the Prayer Book, and the Formularies of the Church whose offices they held. One of their number accepted a Bishopric, and an offer of the same office was made to others, including Richard Baxter.

Some of them were instituted as chaplains of the new monarch.

All this goes to shew that the authorities of the Church did not act in a high-handed manner, but were anxious for conciliation and compromise. Nor is this all.

It is neccesary to enquire what had been the attitude and conduct of those organizations, represented by these 2,000 ministers—the Presbyterians and Independents—toward the Church?

They had beheaded the King, and the Archbishop of Canterbury. They had displaced every Bishop, and wantonly despoiled or infamously profaned every Cathedral They had made even the private use of the Prayer Book a crime, and had driven by no less than 30,000 persons from the parsonages which were their rightful homes. They had decided that no ejected clergyman should be allowed to earn his living as a schoolmaster, either in public or private, and had filled the jails, castles, and ship hulks, with offending clergy, to be left for long periods without trial and justice Very much may be said in extenuation of these facts for this was a wild fierce age, when no party understood the claims of mutual forbearance But, in the face of such facts it certainly cannot be said to be an injustice and wrong when 1,200* of these intruders were asked, with an alternative, to give up the livings they had usurped and to which they had no kind of claim.

---

* Not 2,000

APPENDIX H.

The custom of "House-marks"

See p. 57 and the illustration opposite that page.

On the grave stone of Cuthbert Watson there are three devices The tradition, as indicated on p. 58, is that these are his "marks."

Some light is thrown upon this by an item in The Paine Roll.

Towards the end of The Roll we have this :—
"That no man shall mark any other man's mark upon paine of six shillings and eight pence, but to mark and keep his own house marks."

It has been shewn that in the old home of the English, between the Elbe and the Eider, the owner's mark was cut in stone over the principal door of his house. "It designated not only his land and cattle, but his stall in Church, and his grave " when he died.

This custom of the "house mark" was introduced into this district by the early settlers *

Mr. Wallace, in his MS. notes, ventures the opinion that some of these ancient marks may be discovered on the older gravestone at Alston and Garrigill.

There can be little doubt that the grave stone of Cuthbert Watson, in the Vestry of Garrigill Church, preserves a record of this character.

---

* Vide Williams, in Archaeologia, Vol 37. p. 371. Also Nanson, in Cumberland and Westmoreland Transactions, Vol. 8, pt. 1.

APPENDIX J.

John Archer.

See p. 159.

I have thought it well to present the authority for the statement re John Archer. The following is from Surtees Soc. Pub., vol. 56, p. 229 :—

Archbishop Gray's (or Grey) Register Pt. II., MCCXXVIII, 16 Kal Martii XIII

"A grant to John le Archer, his heir, and assignees, 'exceptis viris religiosis', for his homage and service, of 40 acres of our waste land at 'Hextold,' within these bounds, 'de Bedelech versus occid. ultra Leyam usque Gressiwelle—heued ; et sic usque Greystan, et sic de Greystan usque Wateresweli ; et sic usque Withemeleche ; et sic descendendo usque in Blindeburn ; et sic versus or sicut Blindeburn se extendit usque ad sepes de Milhop; et sic juxta illas sepes in longitudine usque in Dedeleche juxta Hauekestan', cum omnibus aisiamentis et communia de Ninebenkes. Rent a mark of silver per ann."

There is an interesting suggestion as to the *origin* of this name in Testa. de Neville sive Liber Feodorum in Curia Scaccarii Temp. Hen. iii et Edw. I. Escheat 20 Edward iii (1347) No 6: John le Archer held the day of his death, one messuage and four acres of land in Yapam or Yarom, of the king *in Capite*, by the seventh part of a certain serjeanty, which entire serjeanty is held of the king *in Capite*, *by finding one man with bow and arrows* in the Castle of York.

APPENDIX K.

LANDS OF THE PRIOR AND CONVENT OF HEXHAM.
See Preface.

From *Memorials of Hexham*, vol. ii, *The Black Book*, p 20 :—

" GERARD-GILL.

Tenent etiam in Gerard-Gill unum toftum quod vocatur Thruswell, et pasturam ibidem ad x vaccas et duas equas cum tota sequela sua duorum annorum."

" PRESDALE *

Tenent etiam totum Presdale, et est seperale omni tempore anni ; et, si quis depascuerit cum bestiis aliquibus aliquo tempore infra divisas pasturae de Presdale, debet attachiari ad curiam Prioris ibidem et justificari

Et continetur infra has divisas :—

Incipiendo sub Esgy-heued, sicut aqua coelestis dividit usque Edestan : et inde usque Burnhop-heuyde per Hard-rode, sicut aqua dividit, usque Broun-spot-lane ; et inde usque le Crokyt-burn-heued ; et per dictum Crokit-burn usque in aquam de Tese, et sic ab ingressu del Crokit-burne in Tese ascendendo usque in summitatem de Fendes-fell ; et exinde directe usque Wak-stan-eghe, et inde usque fontem de Kex-bur-wane, et exinde usque Grosgil-heued ; et inde, ex transverso mussae, versus or. usque Ninistanes ; et deinde usque Cokeley-fell, et exinde, descendendo per Ellir-burne, usque in aquam de Tyna ; et sic per Tynam usque in Esk-gil-fote ; et exinde, ascendendo per Esk-gille, usque Esk-gille-heuede prius nominatum.

---

* Presdale is now known in part as Priorsdale

Habent etiam liberum ingressum, transitum, et
exitum per totum feodum de Aldestone ad praedictum
Presdale, sine impedimento alicujus, et ad homines
praedictorum PRIORIS et CONVENTUS, et ad omnia
genera animalium suorum · nec calumpnientur vel
vexentur, sive in redeundo vel transeundo, moram
faciendo die vel nocte in pastura de Aldenestone cum
averiis suis extra divisas de Presdale prius nominatas.
Et praedicti PRIOR et CONVENTUS habent communicar'
per totam pasturam de Aldeneston-more cum omnibus
animalibus suis exeuntibus de Presdale, singulis
diebus, pro beneplacito suo, a solis ortu usque ad
occasum, absque contradictione cujuscumque."

"LIBERTATES ET AYSIAMENTA AD PRESDALE IN ALDENESTON-MORE.

Habent etiam, praedicti Prior et Conventus et eorum
homines in villa de Aldneston manentes, in boscis de
Aldneston estoveria ad aedificandum, et ad domos et ad
sepes suas sustinendas, et ad omnia alia necessaria,
prout opus habuerint sine contradictione cujuscumque.

Tenent etiam in villa Chestrehope in Redesdale
ij tofta et ij crofta Quae quidem crofta cum toftis
jacent adinvicem, quia in medio villae, ex austr. parte
le ford, in le peth quod ducit ad communam pasturae,
jac. ex parte bor. dictae peth : et duas bovatas
vocatas j husband-land cont. di. acr. ut caeterae
terrae husband in eadem villa, scilicet xxiiij acras.
Et jacebant vastae fere per XL annos : et dimittuntur
omnia adinvicem in grosso ad terminum x annorum,
reddendo inde annuatim xs. Et inde remittuntur
Adae de Lee, tenenti eorundem, per Priorem, pro bono
consilio suo et servitio, quolibet anno durante termino
praedictorum x annorum vjs viiijd. Et sic solvit de
claro per eosdem annos iijs iiijd."

APPENDIX L.

THE FAMILY OF RENWICK
See Preface.

It was my intention to include these notes in Chapters xviii. and xix , but enquiries on some points delayed the matter too long.

The Renwicks have been in Garrigill for three hundred and fifty years at least, and the sources of information about this family are somewhat varied.

The Paine and Drift Rolls, the Church Registers, the Register of Redwing Meeting House, the Wardens' Accounts, and the family papers all supply interesting items. For the abstracts from the Redwing Register I am indebted to the esteemed courtesy of the Rev. T C. Crosby, Congregational Minister, of Alston.

There is an interesting reference to one member of the family in the Drift Roll of 1597.

Item.—" The Tenements of Nether Cragge shall drive over at the foot of Guddergill and so to Lortburn, and so to the Black Syke, and so to the ffell   And in Winter in ffrost and snow to drive over Tyne through the head of Richard Renwick ffield, and when he breaks the Dyke every year to pay fourpence."

In 1768 John Renwick was Church Warden, and since that date different members of the family have occupied the office about twenty times.

From 1788 to 1814 an excellent account of the family is preserved by Joseph Renwick and his wife " Malle " (Mally for Mary).

The Renwicks at this time were Dissenters, and the Baptism and Burial Register at Redwing Chapel contains many references to the family.

The following are disconnected items from the Church Register :—

1. In 1707 Frances Renwick was buried in Garrigill Churchyard

2. In 1723 and 1724 another Richard Renwick buried his daughter and wife respectively in the same place.

3. William Robson and Anne Renwick, both of this parish, were married 21st August, 1746.

4 Jonathan Kidd of the parish of Stanhope, and Ann Renwick of this parish, were married in this church by Banns, with the consent of their parents, this 10th day of May, 1757, by me, Thomas Lancaster, Vicar of Alston. This marriage was solemnized between us. Jonathan Kidd. Ann Renwick, now Ann Kidd. In the presence of John Kidd, John Renwick.

5. John Craig and Elizabeth Renwick, both of this parish, were married in this church by Banns, this 16th day of May, 1765, by me. Thos. Lancaster, Vicar. This marriage was solemnized between us. John Craig. Elizabeth Renwick, now Craig. In the presence of Jacob Vipond, Isaac Vipond.

6. John, son of William and Judith Renwick of Dryburn, was baptized December 30th, 1779.

7. Mary and Elizabeth, daughters of William Renwick of Dryburn, were baptized March 19th, 1772.

8. Richard Renwick of Ashgill buried June 4, 1739.

9. Hannah, daughter of John and Mary Renwick Eskgill, was buried September 23rd, 1762.

From about 1730 I am able to construct, using all available sources of information, a consecutive table of one line.

JOHN RENWICK OF PRIOR'S DALE.

JOHN	JOSEPH	HENRY	HANNAH	WILLIAM
Bap Jan 26, 1730	Bap Sept 11, 1733	Bap May 13, 1736	Bap Oct 12, 1738	Bap May 22, 1741

JOSEPH RENWICK (aged 55) was married to Mary Dodd (aged 30), on Tuesday, July 22, 1788, by Thomas Lancaster, Vicar of Alston (see p 38), at Garrigill Church The witnesses were Thomas Craig, George Dodd, and Robert Bell Joseph died January 7, 1800 Redwing Register says he was 65 (? 67) Timothy Nelson the dissenting minister preached his funeral sermon from Ep Heb ix. 27, no doubt suggested by the motto in the family Bible.—

"Remember man that dye thou must,
And after that to judgment just."

The entry of his death is made in the family records by the widow's own hand She adds this prayer "Lord, rest his soul in heaven !" When her daughter "Mally" died, she again makes the entry of the death, and repeats *mutatis mutandis* the same pious ejaculation It is interesting and pleasing to see that the matron of this nonconformist household could let her prayers follow her beloved dead Mary Renwick died March, 1838 Redwing Register says she was 84 (? 80)

JOSEPH RENWICK Married Ann Cowper, Dec 30, 1731

HENRY	JOSEPH
Born June 8, 1732	Born Nov 22, 1734

JOSEPH
Married Ann ("Nancy" or "Nanny") Bell
Born May 12, 1789, Baptised May 24, 1789, Buried Aug 15, 1855
"He was a faithful man I have worshipped with him at Redwing Meeting-house about 40 years."
Written by Jonathan Harper in the Redwing Register.

HENRY
("Harry") Married Mary ——. Born Aug 18, 1791.

"MALLY"
Born May 7 1793. Baptised June 7, 1793.
(The Redwing Register says she was born May 18, and baptised June 3)
Married John Richardson of Eskgill, April 24, 1813. Died in childbed, June 11, 1814, aged 21.

JOHN
Born Nov 5, 1797
Married Mary Watson, of Crossgill.

There is a very curious entry by Joseph Renwick concerning his four children during a visitation of smallpox :—
"In the month of January, and in the year of our Lord, 1798, I, Joseph Renwick of Eskgillside, got all my four children inoculated for the smallpox, by Dr Burton of Alston . Paid the Doctor 8s for inoculating and attendance
"And now, blessed be the name of the Lord God Almighty, who hath safely brought my children all through the troubles of the smallpox !" Feb. 20, 1798

John died aged 52, Oct. 18, 1849.

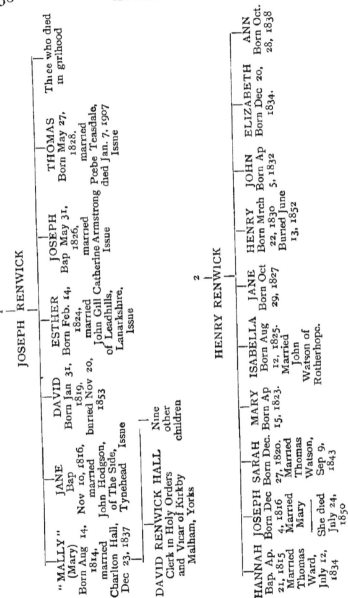

JOSEPH RENWICK

"MALLY" (Mary) Born Aug 14, 1814, married Charlton Hall, of The Side, Tynehead Dec 23, 1837

JANE Bap Nov 10, 1816, married John Hodgson, Issue

DAVID Born Jan 31, 1819, buried Nov 20, 1853

ESTHER Born Feb. 14, 1824, married John Gill of Leadhills, Lanarkshire, Issue

JOSEPH Bap May 31, 1826, married Catherine Armstrong Issue

THOMAS Born May 27, 1828, married Pœbe Teasdale, died Jan. 7, 1907 Issue

Three who died in girlhood

DAVID RENWICK HALL Clerk in Holy Orders and Vicar of Kirkby Malham, Yorks

Nine other children

HENRY RENWICK

HANNAH Bap. Ap. 21, 1815 Married Thomas Ward, July 12, 1834

JOSEPH Born Dec 4, 1816 Married Mary She died July 24, 1850

SARAH Born Dec. 27, 1820, Married Thomas Watson, Sep 9, 1843

MARY Born Ap 15, 1823.

ISABELLA Born Aug 12, 1825. Married John Watson of Rotherhope.

JANE Born Oct 29, 1827

HENRY Born Mrch 22, 1830 Buried June 13, 1852

JOHN Born Ap 5, 1832

ELIZABETH Born Dec 20, 1834.

ANN Born Oct. 28, 1838

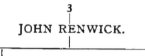

3
JOHN RENWICK.

JANE
Born Oct 28, 1825
Married William Thomason

ISABELLA
Born Aug 3, 1827
Married William Gill of Ivy House,
Dec 3, 1850

APPENDIX M.

See Preface.

THE LANDS OF THE PRIOR AND CONVENT OF HEXHAM.

From Memorials of Hexham, vol ii, p. 113 (The Charter of King Edward I.) :—

"Tenent etiam quandam pasturam, quae vocatur Presdale, cum suis pertinentiis, per suas rectas divisas, in suo separali, in liberam, puram, et perpetuam elemosinam, de dono Ivonis de Veteri-ponte; et inde habuerunt cartam et confimationem domini regis H. patris domini regis nunc; et tenuerunt a tempore quo non extat memoria.

APPENDIX N.

Garrigill Chapelry may fairly claim to have some literary associations.

1. In addition to Westgarth Forster's *Strata* *
several books of more than local interest are intimately
associated with Garrigill.

2. The Game Laws and the thorny question of
poaching do not come within the scope of this book.

But the subject was made the basis of a brief
religious story about a century ago. The authoress was
a sister of Westgarth Forster—Phœbe, who married
Thomas Brown †

The book is thus described by its own title
page :—

"Emma or the Miner's Cottage, a moral tale,
founded on the recent adventures of the poachers,
and the attempts of the Soldiers and Constables to
take them in Alston-moor in 1819. Alston, Cumberland. Printed at the Geological Press, and sold by
John Pattinson, 1821. Price Eighteenpence."

3. Miss James of Clarghyll Hall, a prolific
writer, daughter of the Rev. Octavius James, Curate-in-
charge of Garrigill (1841-2), has written a most delight-
ful story, the scene of which is placed in this village. It
it is a faithful and sympathetic picture of the lives of

---

* Vide p 177   † Vide p 178.

the people. The book is entitled " A pearl in the shell," and Miss James writes under the *nom-de-plume* of Austin Clare.

4. The acknowledged local history is the product of the pen of William Wallace :—

" Alston Moor, its pastoral people : its Mines and Miners. From the earliest periods to recent times. Newcastle, 1890."

Mr. Wallace was intimately connected with Garrigill. I find this interesting note in his MS. :

" My great-great-grandfather Richard Wallace who died in 1773 may have known Reginald Walton. Mrs. E. Millican who resided at Tynehead could recollect Richard Wallace her grandfather.

The three lives comprehend the period from James I. to 14 Victoria."

5. The Rev. William Nall, M.A., who edited Westgarth Forster's *Strata* * was Curate of Alston from 1877 to 1890, and also officiated at Garrigill.

He wrote an excellent handbook also to Alston and its neighbourhood.

6 The publication of The Garrigill Register is referred to on page 99.

---

* Vide p. 177.

GENERAL INDEX.

Aidan, St , 22

Alston, Advowson, xix, 23 , Coroner of
xxiii , The prison at, 19 , Registers, 99 ;
Greek entry, 101 , Latin entry, 100 ;
Vicars of, 23, 24, 26

Archer, the first name in the Burial
Register, 158 , his pedigree, 162, 163 ,
Rowbotham's account, 158-161 , John,
229

Augustine, St , of Canterbury, 21

Bell, The Church, a Legend concerning,
60

Benefactions
Atwood, Charles, 150
Brown, Forster, *vide* Postscript
Emerson, Catherine, 151 note, 208-212
Fairhill Estate, 136
Shield, John, 133
Stephenson, John, 146
Unknown donor, 149
Wilkinson, Robert, 134

Biographies
Forster, Westgarth, 177
Hurst, Blyth, 180
Shield, Joseph, 184
Taylor, John, 173

Black Book of Hexham, The, x

Blacklock, John, 110

Blencarne, 107

Brampton, 188

Brengewenne, Hugh, Vicar of Alston, 24

Bruce, Dr , 2

Burnand, Nathaniel, 188, The will of, 196

Butts, The, at Garrigill, 171, 215

Calamy, quoted, 188

Candida Casa, 21

Census, 216, *et seq.*

Chapelry, The origin of the, 25, 26

Chaplain, 26, 201

Chest of iron for documents, 95

Chesters, Tynehead, 2

Christmas, 215

Church, The, at Garrigill, Early repairs of,
xxii, 32-35, also *sub* John Archer, 163 ;
Bell, 61 , Communion Vessels, 64 ;
Eagle Lectern, 65 , Eucharistic Lights,
65 , Font, The, 67-70 , East and South
Windows, 46 , Gallery erected, 30 ,
Organ added, 47 , Pewter Vessels, 62 ,
Porch, 50 , Reconstruction, 41-48 ,
Seats appropriated, 30-32 , Vestry
added, 53 , Weather Vane, 52 ; West
Window, 49

Churchwardens, xxii, The duties of, 72 ;
List of the, 75-84 , Mode of election,
71-72 , Privileges of the, 73 , Tenement
election ceases, 85 , Warned by the
Archdeacon, 131

Church Room, 50, 58

Churchyard, The, 47 , Cross socket, 112 ,
Curious custom, 113 , Enlarged, 109 ,
Early burials, 107 , North side of the,
111-112 , Gates of the, 48 , Theory by
William Wallace, 102-105 , Wallace
criticised, 105-109

Clergy, The list of, 37-39

Clocker, John and Joseph, 150

Coins, found in Garrigill, 2

Congregationalism, 191-195 ; Magazine
quoted, 196-198

Constables, The Village, 86 , Balance
sheet of, 86 , Elected by the Vestry, 86 ,
Elected by the Manor Court, 89 , List
of, 87

Corbridge, Fair at, 201

Coroner, xxiii

Cowper, Stephen, Schoolmaster, 116

Cross Fell, xvii-xviii

Cross, The Village, 112

Culgaith, 107

Cumberland, Why Garrigill is in, 28

Dawes, Thomas, 196

Davy, John, 191

Dean, John, 197

LIST OF PATRONS AND SUBSCRIBERS

————:-o-:————

Deceased Patrons marked—*   *Some Patrons have taken several copies.*

————:-o-:————

THE LORDS COMMISSIONERS OF THE ADMIRALTY.

THE RT HON THE LORD BARNARD, D.C.L , Raby Castle, Darlington.

* THE RT. REV. E. R. WILBERFORCE, D.D., The Lord Bishop of Chichester (Formerly of Newcastle).

* THE RIGHT REV. ARTHUR T. LLOYD, D D., The Lord Bishop of Newcastle

THE RT. REV. N. D. J STRATON, D.D., The Lord Bishop of Newcastle

THE RIGHT REV. EDGAR JACOB, D.D , The Lord Bishop of St. Albans.

* THE VENERABLE ARCHDEACON HAMILTON, D.D.

THE VENERABLE ARCHDEACON HENDERSON, M.A.

ADAMSON, L. W. ESQ , LL D., Linden, Lucy Horsley, R S O.

ANDERSON, NICHOLAS, MR., Tynehead, Garrigill.

ARCHER, MARK, ESQ., Farnacres, Ravensworth.

ARCHER, JOSEPH, ESQ., Ashville, Rothbury.

ARMSTRONG, GEORGE, MR., Ashgill, Garrigill.

BARKER, ERNEST, ESQ , London

BARKER, VERNON, ESQ , London.

BELL, W. HEWARD, ESQ , Seend, Wiltshire.

BLACKBURN, EDWARD, ESQ , Haltwhistle.

* BROWN, T FORSTER, ESQ , Bristol.

BUSHBY, JACOB, MR , Ivy House, Garrigill.

CARSON, STEWART, ESQ , Salvin Lodge, Alston

CLIPPINGDALE, S D , ESQ , M D., Holland Park Avenue, W.

COOK, H ESQ., Newcastle-on-Tyne

CROSBY, THOMAS, C THE REV , Craig House, Alston.

DUKINFIELD-ASTLEY, H J., THE REV , Litt. D. , F.R. Hist, S.; F R S L , The Vicarage, East Rudham.

ELLIOT ROBERT, ESQ , The Bank, Alston.

FERGUSON, S C MAJOR, 37 Lowther Street, Carlisle

FISHER, JOSEPH, ESQ., Higham, Bassenthwaite Lake, Cockermouth

GILL, CHRISTOPHER, C ESQ , Bath

* GREENWELL, JONATHAN, MR , Garrigill.

HALL, THE REV. DAVID RENWICK, Kirkby Malham Vicarage

HALL, JOHN, MR , Windy Hall, Garrigill.

HALL, CHARLTON, MR , School House, Gilsland.

HESLOP, R. OLIVER, M A , F S A , Eskdale Terrace, Newcastle-on-Tyne

HEWITT, SOUTHBY, ESQ , Cadogan Place, S.W.

HODGSON, JOSEPH, MR., Bayle Hill, Alston.

HORROCKS, R. H. ESQ., Salkeld Hall, Langwathby.

* HORROCKS, THOMAS, ESQ , Eden Brows, Amathwaite.

HUNSIKER, MILLARD, COLONEL, Cornhill, E.C.

INGLEDOW, W. C. THE REV., Rector of Knaresdale.

JAMES, MISS, W. M., Clarghyll Hall, Alston.

JOICEY, EDWARD, ESQ , Blenkinsopp, Haltwhistle

KERSEY, W E ESQ , Felixstowe

LEE, PERCY T , THE REV., M A., The Vicarage, Shilbottle, Lesbury R S O

LOWE, THE REV. CANON, M A , R D., Haltwhistle.

MONKHOUSE, C ESQ , Fairfield, Stanhope, R S O

MYLNE, R. S., THE REV , M A , B C.L (OXON), F S A., F.R S , (Scotland) Rector of Furthoe.

PICKERING, MRS., ADAM, Garrigill.

RENWICK, JOHN, MR., Crossgill, Garrigill.

RENWICK, JOSEPH, MR , Lord Crewe Arms, Blanchland.

RICHARDSON, J. J. MR , Garrigill.

RICHARDSON, JOSEPH, MR , Garrigill.

ROBINSON, J W. ESQ , Brokenhaugh, Haydon Bridge

ROWBOTHAM, G. H. ESQ , Chorlton-cum-Hardy

RUSTON-HARRISON, C. W. ESQ., 8 Eden Terrace, Stanwix

RUTHERFORD, THE REV W. A , D.D., R N , Penrith.

SAVAGE, THE REV. CANON, M A , The Vicarage, Halifax

SHIELD, MISS, HARRIET, Garrigill.

TODD, R. ESQ , The Raise, Alston.

WALTON, ISAAC, ESQ., Newington Causeway.

WALTON, J. R. ESQ , J.P., Lowbyer, Alston.

WALTON, HENRY, ESQ , J P , The Raise, Alston.

WALTON, T Mr., Howburn, Garrigill

WALKER, THE REV. JOHN, M A., Whalton Rectory.

WELFORD, RICHARD, ESQ , M A., F.R A.S , Gosforth,

WESTGARTH, T THE REV , The Parsonage, Garrigill

WIGLEY, J. M. MR , Lancaster

WILSON, J W WALTON, ESQ , Shotley Hall, Northumberland

WOOD, HERBERT MAXWELL, ESQ., 3 Manor Place, Sunderland

* VIPOND, JAMES, MR., Garrigill.

VIPOND, JAMES, MR., Silverdale, Chelmsford.

VIPOND, PETER, MR., Gallow Shield Rigg, Bardon Mill.

VIPOND, SARAH, MISS, Plumstead, Kent.

LIBRARIES AND INSTITUTIONS.

THE BRITISH MUSEUM

THE UNIVERSITY LIBRARY, CAMBRIDGE.

TRINITY COLLEGE LIBRARY, DUBLIN.

THE PUBLIC LIBRARY, TULLIE HOUSE, CARLISLE per L E. Hope, Esq

THE REFERENCE LIBRARY, MANCHESTER, per Charles W Sutton Esq

CHEETHAM'S LIBRARY, HUNTS BANK, MANCHESTER, per Walter T. Brown Esq

THE SOCIETY OF ANTIQUARIES, NEWCASTLE-ON-TYNE, per Robert Blair, Esq, F S A.

THE LITERARY & PHILOSOPHICAL SOCIETY, NEWCASTLE-ON-TYNE, per Henry Richardson, Esq.

THE PUBLIC LIBRARY, NEWCASTLE-ON-TYNE, per Basil Anderton, Esq, B.A.

THE PUBLIC LIBRARY, WIGAN, Per F Folkard, Esq., F.S A.

THE PUBLIC LIBRARIES, LEEDS, per Thomas W. Hand, Esq.

THE CHURCH READING ROOM, GARRIGILL.

AMERICA.

The Subscribers in America are not in this List.

When this last sheet was going through the press I was pleased to get the following note from the Revd. T. Westgarth. It is both interesting and valuable :—

"DEAR MR. CAINE,

1. You will be delighted to hear that I have found in Garrigill a Holy Water Stoup! The man engaged in laying the pipes for the Garrigill Water Supply turned it up, and gave it to the person with whom he was staying, who on being told what it was readily gave it to be restored to the Church.

I may mention that this relic and the ancient Font you had re-erected are made of the same kind of stone.

The stoup will be placed on a stone bracket on the west wall, and just behind the font.

We cannot identify the exact spot where it was found As a drain was cut the whole length of the Churchyard wall, it is probable that it was brought to light there.

2. A legacy of £250 has been left by the late Forster Brown of Bristol to be invested by the Vicar of Alston for the benefit of the poor of Garrigill.

3 We have now entered upon the entire renovation of our dear old Church, and we expect to have our re-opening service about Whitsuntide.

Very sincerely yours,
T. WESTGARTH."